TWAYNE'S WORLD AUTHORS SERIES
A Survey of the World's Literature

FRANCE

EDITOR

Maxwell A. Smith, Guerry Professor of French, Emeritus
The University of Chattanooga
Former Visiting Professor in Modern Languages
The Florida State University

Barbey D'Aurevilly

TWAS 468

Barbey D'Aurevilly

BARBEY D'AUREVILLY

By ARMAND B. CHARTIER

University of Rhode Island

TWAYNE PUBLISHERS
A DIVISION OF G. K. HALL & CO., BOSTON

Library of Congress Cataloging in Publication Data

Chartier, Armand B.
  Barbey d'Aurevilly.

  (Twayne's world authors series; TWAS 468: France)
  Bibliography: p. 177–79.
  Includes index.
  1. Barbey d'Aurevilly, Amédée, 1808-1889—Criticism and
interpretation.
  PQ2189.B32Z656   848'.8'09   77-8024
  ISBN 0-8057-6305-8

To Monique, Marc, and Bernard,
this gentle reminder of their
French heritage

Contents

About the Author

Armand B. Chartier was born in New Bedford, Massachusetts. He holds diplomas from Assumption College and from the University of Massachusetts. He is presently a member of the Department of Languages at the University of Rhode Island, where he teaches courses on Realism, Symbolism and Québécois literature.

Active in many ethnic organizations, he serves on the American and Canadian French Cultural Exchange Commission (State of Rhode Island) and on the Council for the Development of French in New England. An Editor of *Modern Language Studies,* he is also a member of the Executive Council of the Northeast Modern Language Association and of the Committee on Bibliography of the Modern Language Association. He has published in the fields of Québécois literature and Franco-American literature and is project Co-ordinator for the Comprehensive History of Ethnic Literature planned by the Society for the Study of the Multi-Ethnic Literature of the United States.

Preface

The Comte Robert de Montesquiou-Fezensac found Barbey d'Aurevilly so formidable that he never summoned up the courage to express to him personally the deep admiration he felt for him. Others, such as Léon Bloy and Paul Bourget, were more fortunate in that they were allowed to approach the Master, benefiting from his advice and encouragement. Most of his contemporaries dismissed him as an eccentric or as a paradox, for they were unable to reconcile the boldness of his novels with the reactionary religious and political ideas he kept reiterating during a half-century as a literary critic. After being relegated to a literary limbo for many years, Barbey today enjoys a better reputation than ever before. Readers are less drawn to the impassioned, controversial critic, than to the author of "strange" fictions, in which he excels in conjuring up personal holocausts and cataclysms. Underlying these stories lie a complexity and a profoundly anguished, tragic vision of life, not yet thoroughly analyzed, despite much recent progress in that direction.

The present work barely hints at that fascinating complexity. After a biographical sketch, the reader will find a short chapter on dandyism, a modest attempt to define that phenomenon and to indicate its place in Barbey's life and works. Chapter Three deals with four novels which occupy a central place within the entire corpus. In Chapter Four, I discuss each of the *Diaboliques* — his unquestioned masterpiece — and the last two novels he published. His literary criticism is given short shrift in Chapter Five, because his fiction remains vastly more important than his criticism. Space has not permitted a discussion of "Le cachet d'onyx" or "Léa," his first short stories, which eventually became two of his *Diaboliques*.

This study assumes no previous knowledge of Barbey on the part of the reader. Should this study increase the number of Barbey's readers, I would be most gratified ... and I would envy those readers the pleasures of their discovery.

ARMAND B. CHARTIER

Kingston. Rhode Island

Acknowledgments

The lamented Reverend Polyeucte Guissard, A.A., of Assumption College, is responsible for my "discovery" of Barbey d'Aurevilly, and without the promptings of our beloved "Père Polyeucte," this book might never have been written. The book also owes much to Professor Seymour S. Weiner of the University of Massachusetts, whose love and knowledge of writers such as Barbey are likely to inspire his present and former students for the next several decades. My colleagues Professors Thomas D. Morin, Constantin Toloudis and Harold A. Waters have offered many helpful suggestions and I should like to thank them here. My thanks also go to the Department of Languages of the University of Rhode Island, and in particular to our past Chairmen, Professors Ruth H. Kossoff and Henry F. Capasso, for their constant encouragement. A word of gratitude is due to Professor Nathaniel M. Sage, Coordinator of Research, who generously subsidized the preparation of the final draft. I am much indebted to Professor Jacques Petit, whose countless publications have contributed greatly to my understanding of Barbey's life and works. Without the prodigious patience and trust of Professors Sylvia E. Bowman and Maxwell A. Smith, someone else would have had the privilege of writing the Barbey book for Twayne, and to them I also extend my most gracious thanks.

Finally, I must acknowledge my special indebtedness to Professor Paul-P. Chassé of Rhode Island College, who offered not only sound advice on technical matters, but much moral support as well.

Chronology

Publication dates are listed for the more significant works only. The dates indicate the first appearance in volume form.

1808   November 2, birth of Jules-Amédéé Barbey at Saint-Sauveur-le-Vicomte in Normandy. Early education probably received at nearby Collège de Valognes.

1827   Attends the Collège Stanislas in Paris; becomes friends with Maurice de Guérin. Discovers Byron and Scott.

1829   Enters Law School at Caen.

1830-   Liaison with Louise Cantru des Costils. Begins long friend-
1831   ship with the scholar Guillaume-Stanislas Trébutien. Writes his first short story, "Le cachet d'onyx" ("The Onyx Seal"), not published until 1919.

1832   "Léa."

1833-   Settles in Paris. Writes *La Bague d'Annibal* ("Hannibal's
1835   Ring") and his first novel, *Germaine ou La pitié,* published in 1883 as *Ce qui ne meurt pas (What Never Dies).*

1836-   Struggles to earn a living as a social and literary critic, con-
1840   tributing to various newspapers. Discovers Joseph de Maistre and Stendhal. Frequents the Catholic, royalist salon of Madame Almaury de Maistre.

1841   *L'Amour impossible.*

1845   *Du dandysme et de G. Brummell.*

1846-   Intellectual return to Catholicism. Becomes editor of the
1848   short-lived *Revue du Monde Catholique.*

1850   Publishes articles in *La Mode,* a legitimist newspaper, and "Le dessous de cartes d'une partie de whist," the first of the *Diaboliques.*

1851   *Une vieille maîtresse; Les prophètes du passé.* Meets the Baronne de Bouglon to whom he later becomes engaged, but whom he never married.

1852   Supports Louis-Napoléon. Begins a lengthy association with *Le Pays,* a Bonapartist newspaper.

1854   *L'Ensorcelée* ("The Bewitched"). Meets Baudelaire with whom he remained friendly for several years.

1855   Resumes the practice of his Catholic faith.

1857   Defends *Les Fleurs du Mal* on moral and esthetic grounds.

1858   Co-founder of *Le Réveil,* a Catholic newspaper which staunchly supports the government of Napoleon III. End of friendship with Trébutien.

1860   First volume of *Les Oeuvres et les Hommes,* a collection of his articles.

1862-   His polemical articles win him more enemies than friends.
1863

1864   *Le Chevalier des Touches.*

1865   *Un prêtre marié* ("A Married Priest"). His articles are accepted by *Le Nain Jaune,* despite this newspaper's anti-clerical nature.

1867-   Meets Léon Bloy. Replaces Sainte-Beuve as a literary critic
1871   of *Le Constitutionnel.* After the Siege of Paris, returns to Normandy and completes the *Diaboliques.* Almost every year until his death, he will spend some time in Normandy.

1872   Meets François Coppée.

1874   November: *Les Diaboliques.* December: Prosecution begins.

1875   The charges are dismissed after Barbey agrees to end the sale of the *Diaboliques.*

1876   Meets Paul Bourget who will soon become an admirer, as will other young writers, including Huysmans, Lorrain, Péladan, Richepin, and Rollinat.

1877   *Les Bas-bleus* ("The Bluestockings") is read as an anti-feminist work.

1879   Meets Louise Read who will become a devoted secretary and will oversee the posthumous publication of several volumes, including many in the series *Les Oeuvres et les Hommes.*

1880-   *Goethe et Diderot.* 1882: *Une histoire sans nom (A Story*
1885   *Without a Name).* 1883: Partial publication of his personal journal *(Memoranda)* with a preface by Paul Bourget. 1884: writes his last articles of literary criticism (on Bloy, Richepin, Huysmans and Péladan). 1885: resumes publication of *Les Oeuvres et les Hommes.*

1886 "Une page d'histoire." *Sensations d'art.*
1887 *Sensations d'histoire.*
1888 Falls seriously ill.
1889 *Les Poètes* (Constitutes Vol. 11 of *Les Oeuvres et les Hommes*). April 23: Death of Barbey d'Aurevilly.

CHAPTER 1

Biographical Sketch

I *Early Years*

JULES-Amédée Barbey — later Barbey d'Aurevilly — was born on November 2, 1808, in Saint-Sauveur-le-Vicomte in Normandy. Had he been born a few hours earlier, his birth date would have been All Saints' Day, a day of jubilation when the Church celebrates the memory of all those who are presumed to have entered the Kingdom of Heaven. But November 2 is All Souls' Day, when celebration gives way to a spirit of sack-cloth and ashes, when the emphasis shifts from Eternal Reward to a rather melancholy meditation on Death and the uncertainty which follows. The day's significance did not elude Barbey's notice: "I was born on a gloomy, icy winter day, the day of sighs and tears, which the Dead, whose name it bears, have marked with prophetic dust . . . I have always believed that this day would cast a baleful influence on my life and thought."[1]

The Cotentin peninsula, that far-flung and mysterious region of Normandy,[2] was to have an even greater influence on his life and thought. Even a sophisticated tourist like Stendhal admired the setting of the Cotentin (in the Département de la Manche) which, to the perceptive observer, offers a great variety of moods. Along the coast, vast stretches of deserted dunes alternate with inaccessible cliffs. In the interior, marshlands and moors often give way to farms, meadows, wooded districts and secretive hamlets. Even the rains in this region are whimsical and varied. Little wonder that Barbey would find inspiration in both the geography and the climate of his native land.

The people of the Cotentin are no less varied, both in temperament and in type. The Normans' practical sense, their cautiousness and distrust are assuredly as well known as their passion for adventure, which led many of them to the New World as far back as the sixteenth century. The social types which Barbey knew and described are many. They represent every social class, from the arch-royalist aristocratic set of Valognes to the fishermen who abound in local legends and the rich farmers who, in spite of their pragmatism, did not lose their sensitivity for the mysterious and the *fantastique*.

Though deeply influenced by the land and its inhabitants, Barbey was even more affected by his family. Although his family's social status had declined from petty nobility to petty bourgeois, the writer's psychological and spiritual indebtedness to them was great. When he spoke of *his* native land, for example, no one could quarrel with the claim, since his paternal ancestors' link with Saint-Sauveur dated back to the fourteenth century. The family had always been respected for its deep roots and its staunch loyalty to monarchy and the Church. From these ancestors, then, he inherited a feudal world-view which divides society into various degrees of masters and servants. This outlook goes far in explaining his future conduct, as we shall see.

As for Barbey's home life, it might be termed just a bit more felicitous than that of Chateaubriand at Combourg. His father, Théophile Barbey, was a morose tyrant filled with rancor over the events of 1789 and after. While the Revolution suppressed the offices and privileges of the nobility, Barbey père would never adapt to these changes, and began forthwith to live in the past. His stubborn refusal to adjust or to compromise accounts in part for his son's intransigence, for his nearly permanent state of exasperation and for his obsessive cult of the past. For Barbey the writer, life was infinitely more livable in the past than in the present. His mother, Ernestine Barbey, née Ango, was more lively and open than her husband. An avid reader of new books, she had a penchant for fleeing from the banality of her existence into a world of solitary walks and unshared reveries. Her passion for card-playing and for entertaining might have enlivened Jules' existence, but she scarred him forever by telling him that she found him ugly.

The boy found distractions from his repressed yearning for his mother's love in the stories told to him by the family maid, Jeanne Roussel, who kept brightly lit the torch of oral tradition. For this woman — and he would never forget his indebtedness to her — acquainted him with the local legends and superstitions which he used so well in his novels. He also delighted in the stories told by older relatives, concerning either a family secret, or a "ténébreuse affaire" involving the local gentry, or stories about the subversive, terroristic activities of the *Chouans,* an arch-royalist and fiercely individualistic group of rebels. Such legends and stories also provided glimpses of a golden age of strength, order and stability, an age in which the monarchy and the aristocracy ruled supreme. So precociously enthralled by this quest for things past, Barbey would soon look even farther back, beyond the era of the aristocracy to an age of heroism and conquest, the age of Vikings and Norsemen, of whom he was arrogantly proud to be a descendant. But no more than a copse is a forest can these musings he said to constitute a happy childhood; they were oases in a desert of political rancor and Jansenism, or better yet, seeds which would yield an abundant harvest in future novels and stories.

II *Education*

The exact circumstances of his early education are a matter of conjecture. It has been established that he lived intermittently with an uncle, Pontas-Duméril, in nearby Valognes. The place seems particularly apt, since Valognes was a provincial Versailles, where the mores of the old aristocracy, with its accent on elegance and good breeding, were very much alive. In later years, Barbey was to look back with greater fondness to Valognes than to Saint-Sauveur. His uncle, Pontas-Duméril, as mayor of Valognes and — especially — as a medical doctor became privy to local secrets, many of which were transmitted to Barbey — providing more raw material for his writing. Pontas-Duméril also awakened in him a curiosity about medical and physiological anomalies and these phenomena too were to find a place in future works. Finally, Pontas-Duméril was a freethinker and a liberal in politics, and under his tutelage, Barbey was to become both for several years.

After completing his undergraduate studies at the Collège Stanislas in Paris, where a deep friendship developed with the poet Maurice de Guérin, Barbey returned to Saint Sauveur in 1829, vainly seeking his father's permission to begin a career in the military. A bitter quarrel ensued. The elder Barbey's political rancor had not diminished in the least; so Jules, crushed but submissive, followed his father's wishes and went grumbling off to Law School at Caen. Though admittedly not the most scintillating of milieus, Law School did afford the future polemicist the opportunity to develop and strengthen his argumentative tendencies and fostered in him a liking for elaborate systems of thought.

III   *Love and Friendship*

But Barbey had a long memory. Years later, he was still brooding over what might have been: "If, instead of going off to Caen to study law, I had gone saber-rattling in Algeria . . . I would now be a general or I would have been killed. Two good things."[3] Law School notwithstanding, the early eighteen-thirties proved very rich from the standpoint of Barbey's inner life. He fell in love, discovered perfect friendship and wrote two short stories.

During 1830 or 1831, Barbey met and fell passionately in love with Louise Cantru des Costils (recently married to Barbey's cousin), usually referred to as "Elle" or alluded to by suspension points in his personal writings. To date, none of his biographers has been capable of defining precisely the nature of their relationship. Leaving aside the conjectures of various commentators and relying solely upon the few extant documents, it does not appear hyperbolic to state that, at least for Barbey, love came unexpectedly, swiftly and irrevocably. Louise was to become the norm by which her successors were to be measured . . . and by which they failed.

The friend whom Barbey met while in Caen was Guillaume Stanislas Trébutien, an obscure publisher-cum-librarian, an erudite recluse, an ardent admirer and devotee of the phenomenon called Barbey d'Aurevilly long before that phenomenon erupted into the public life of France. The testimony of that twenty-five-year friendship is contained in the four volumes of letters written by Barbey to Trébutien. These letters expressed aspirations and frustrations of every order, from the metaphysical to the financial.

During the early eighteen-thirties, he wrote two erotic horror stories, "Le cachet d'onyx" ("The Onyx Seal"), which remained unpublished until 1919 and "Léa," which appeared in the only issue of *La Revue de Caen,* founded by the author and a small group of friends. The genesis of these stories remains a mystery, but they already afford us glimpses of his lifelong obsession with passion, sex, violence and death.

IV *Paris*

In 1833, having inherited a modest annuity (1200 Francs), Barbey arrived in Paris with all the unused strength and dynamism of his frustrated aristocratic forebears; but he had, for a time, rejected his family's political views. Unspeakably ambitious, he lived beyond his means, confident that royalties would soon make up his budget deficit, confident too that other dreams would be realized. He was certain that the money earned by his writings would allow him to pursue a brilliant political career and to lead an exciting life in the highest social strata. As in his later life, reality was to lag far behind his dreams, even though access to a few salons and newspaper offices led him to believe that success was at hand. The day soon came when he recognized that he could not count on his acquaintances to accelerate his social and professional advancement. His only friend in Paris was Maurice de Guérin who sensitized him to poetry and taught him the value of sincerity. Under his influence, Barbey began writing an intimate journal which he named *Memoranda*.

Whenever he made up his mind to be scrupulous about these journal entries, he was meticulous to the point of tedium in recording his daily activities. He included details about his digestion, the itinerary of his strolls down the boulevards, chance meetings, the number and nature of the drinks he consumed. More to the point, the *Memoranda* reveal a man in quest of himself, in quest too of a position in the world, a man endlessly observing his own actions, a man becoming rapidly disillusioned by an ever-evasive success and dismissing his contemporaries in crisp, definitive summary judgments. Yet one senses beneath the cynical posturing of the dandy and the hollow bombast of the Romantic, the sufferings of a flayed heart and a boredom verging on the metaphysical. One also hears the voice of the moralist, commenting for example on superstition: the least superstitious people are the most mediocre; one cannot be truly distinguished without being superstitious. Further: "... to be superstitious shows that one is capable of deep impressions" (II, 738). As for women, "... they vary only according to the manner in which they yield; once they have yielded, they all resemble one another" (II, 839). Occasionally, one hears a voice which is even more personal and original as when he writes of "... pleasure and pain, two beautiful girls who should be sculptured back to back and bound together by the cincture" (II, 772).

Clearly the dominant theme of Barbey's life in the eighteen-thirties and forties is the polarity delimited by solitude and society. Underlying his ambivalence toward both was a boredom so frequent, so profound, so inescapable that he acknowledged it as the ruling divinity of his life (II, 737). Seeking an absolute in the here and now, Barbey would have found life savorless in any era. If one considers the disproportion between the man and his milieu, his aspirations and the limitations of his age, then one begins to appreciate how paralyzing this sterile sense of universal futility must have been. An aristocrat by instinct, passionate by temperament, he was reduced by circumstances to petty concerns about career and money in the stolid, unexciting Paris of Louis-Philippe, the very bourgeois King of the arch-bourgeois French. A feverish social life was one obvious attempt to escape from this morass; but the result was a love-hate relationship, for he was always breaking with society and forever re-establishing his ties. Society would make him yearn for his room, his books, his papers, but once he had returned to his solitude, he might write: "All evil comes from being alone" (II, 867). As in all else, the land of peace and of his heart's desire is always elsewhere, and he never seems to find whatever he decides to seek.

V *Debut in Journalism*

Converting forced solitude to creative solitude, he sought ballast for his life in reading and note-taking. These unhappy years were also formative years, during which he read voraciously though haphazardly, partly with the aim of preparing for a political career. Historical works, memoirs, law books, all these fell under the rubric of professional preparation. He read treatises on medical questions to satisfy his personal curiosity. Finally, he discovered writers whom he was to admire the remainder of his life: Saint-Simon, Machiavelli, Stendhal, Joseph de Maistre. In the works of the latter, he saw scope and power, a flaming imagination, acuteness of vision and, above all, dazzling beauty and trenchancy of style. Reading de Maistre was a remote preparation for Barbey's return to Catholicism; in fact, he was so taken up by the solid argumentation that one can well wonder why the "return" did not take place sooner. Yet his asceticism was sporadic, forever warring with his violent, contradictory nature, so that we find him reading Byron too and developing a taste for satanism and for passion as blasphemy.

The aimlessness of his life was attenuated in 1838 when he joined the staff of the *Nouvelliste,* founded to uphold the left-center politics of Adolphe Thiers. He wrote erudite articles on law or on the Oriental question, but he found particularly amusing the writing of short polemical articles or drama criticism. Flattered that his articles on the theatre were discussed in certain drawing-rooms, he took special delight in cutting up Victor Hugo's *Ruy Blas.* Such was his debut in a lengthy, tempestuous, erratic career. He was to spend most of his life trying to establish himself as a journalist and he alternately extolled and damned the merits of his profession. His polemical articles betrayed his warrior instincts (always ready to surface) and he often recognized his work for what it really was: a creative escape which provided badly needed cash. He loathed being compelled to set forth opinions he did not share simply in order to safeguard a tenuous position, and he detested having to restrain the contempt in which he held the crass materialism of the times.

Until their falling-out in 1837, Barbey had found a source of strength and encouragement in his Norman friend Trébutien. Factotum, liegeman, he proved a fiercely loyal correspondent and Barbey had begun writing to him frequently in 1834. Self-indulgence, intellectual revelry, stylistic extravaganzas are found on virtually every page of the four volumes called *Lettres à Trébutien.* Nearly every week for a quarter of a century, Barbey sent off a "Dominicale" to his friend in Caen. These are lengthy epistles written in inks of various colors, with the capital letters illuminated in the brightest hues, reminiscent of medieval manuscripts; and certain key words are enhanced by a sprinkle of gold or silver. Much later, Barbey reread them and proclaimed that the *Lettres* would bring him glory; precious as the collection may be for his biographers, they do not constitute a masterpiece, but they do show the man as he would like to be seen: as a tragic hero, oppressed by fate and by the pettiness of the times, but bold, undaunted, strong. In the *Lettres,* Barbey relives his own life; it is indeed a weekly exercise in vicarious re-living, for it pleased him to visualize his life being relived by his sensitive, admiring friend. The hollowness of the flattery which he heaps upon Trébutien and the fiendish pleasure he takes in shocking the prudish recluse were undoubtedly factors in the definitive break which came in 1858. But from 1837 until their reconciliation in 1841, Barbey crossed an emotional desert darkened by the death of Maurice de Guérin, the mysterious loss of his mistress and the decision of his first love, Louise, to end their relationship forever.

VI *The Young Dandy*

Far too proud to bare his wounded heart to a cynical world, convinced that there was nothing more ridiculous than suffering, he used his considerable will power to conceal his sorrows. He would not yield, be it ever so slightly, to the temptation of showing any feeling, except contempt, cultivating instead his need to astound and to shock through irony and scorn. As a caustic wit, he strove to outdo his contemporaries, thus superimposing the mask of the dandy upon that of the stoic. If we also consider his flamboyant manners and dress, it is not always easy to distinguish the mask from the man.

The exact nature of Barbey's dandyism will be dealt with later, but it should be mentioned here that in 1841 he published *L'Amour impossible,* the title of which sums up the effect of love on the dandy. In 1845 he brought out his short essay, *Du dandysme et de G. Brummell* which earned a modest "succès de salon." The paradox of a man fascinated, at the same time, by George Bryan Brummell, the "founder" of dandyism, and Pope Innocent III, the strong-arm medieval pontiff, becomes even more surprising if it is recalled that Byron too figured prominently in Barbey's private pantheon. He found in Byron an idealized version of his own life: lust for action and adventure, exacerbated rebelliousness and dandyism. In fact, he was enthralled by all that Byron represented, whether it be the legendary seducer, the exasperated aristocrat, the criminal, even the poet. All his life he would keep up a fervent cult of Byron, proud to be, in his own estimation, the only Frenchman who knew Byron's works by heart — to within a single comma. This cult is evident in *La Bague d'Annibal* (*Hannibal's Ring,* published in 1844) a short story written in 1834 when Byron's *Don Juan* was in vogue.

By the mid eighteen-forties, "Brummell II" was paddling in the social slush, having become an habitué of the fashionable salon of Madame Almaury de Maistre, a distant relative of Joseph de Maistre. This salon, where he reigned, gave him the social position he had been coveting and was well-suited to his whims and moods which ranged from surly, stone-faced silence to the gusty exuberance of dramatic monologues — tales of sorcery, forbidden love, married priests — abridged versions of future novels. But he received more from Madame de Maistre than a stage and an audience for his dazzling narratives, "sonatas for four hands" performed by himself alone, as he was pleased to report to Trébutien.[4] Indeed we must not underestimate the influence of this Catholic and royalist milieu in the evolution of Barbey's religious and political thought. It is part of a convergence of influences which transformed him for life into a Knight Templar, constantly embattled for the Cross and the Crown.

Meanwhile he went on making Sisyphean efforts to secure a stable position, growing impatient after fame, steadily becoming better known in journalistic and literary circles, though his books did not attract much attention. Encouraged by vague promises of favorable reviews, he haunted chic cafés, Tortoni's or the "Café Anglais" where he might forget his latest "rejection-slip" in the company of Roger de Beauvoir who dazzled everyone with his Scarron-like wit and his cane of rhinoceros horn. He found consolation too with Vellini, a fiery Spanish woman about whom nothing is known except that Barbey remembered her when he needed a *femme fatale* for his first great novel, *Une vieille maîtresse*. The affair was allegedly a diabolical, tempestuous one, but such was the man's love of dramatization and secretiveness both, his eagerness to pass for a rake, that here again he mystifies his biographers.

VII   *Return to Catholicism*

He discovered Balzac around 1845, expressing deep admiration for the latter's Catholicism and monarchist views, for his ideas on societal order and unity. Equally important, Balzac taught him how realism could be combined with the *fantastique*. Thus the reading of Balzac and that of Joseph de Maistre are intimately linked to Barbey's so-called "intellectual" conversion — "intellectual" inasmuch as his return to the faith was chiefly an adherence to Catholic dogma rather than a resumption of Catholic practices.

He soon had the opportunity to publicize his return to Catholicism when he became a co-founder of the short-lived *Revue du Monde Catholique,* largely a propaganda venture which left him a free hand in choosing his topics. Most of the articles concern the political and social role of the Church, since Barbey, sharing Balzac's view of Catholicism, admired the Church's authority principle and viewed the Church mainly as a generative and conservative principle of societies, a rampart against utopians, anarchists, Protestants and other breeders of disorder and revolution.

VIII *Normandy*

Although Pius IX did not become the Louis XVI of the papacy, as indeed Barbey had feared, the Revolution of 1848 confirmed all of Barbey's other fears about the era in which he lived. In the Revolution, he saw and would never forget the vulgarity and self-seeking of his fellow-citizens, the unspeakable baseness and hideousness of the masses. The Revolution, however, was a Parisian phenomenon and a contemporary one. Profoundly repelled, he turned to Normandy where tradition, aristocracy, authority and strength ran so deep they were virtually part of the countryside. Granted, the Norman aristocracy too had suffered a series of severe blows beginning in 1789, and rich, middle-class farmers had replaced the great dukes; but the legends, the tales of heroic exploits were still close at hand, in books which were readily available, or in the oral history related by older folks during Barbey's childhood, and now fondly remembered. He would go on reading medical treatises and histories of Rome, but he would reread Norman history as well: memoirs of dubious authenticity and accounts of the awe-inspiring deeds of the Chouans. The co-operative Trébutien was "mobilized," his research abilities pressed into the service of his friend's new vocation: "I don't want there to be a single Norman name whose history I do not know, and every atom in every pinch of historic dust must be known to me. If I have any genius, it will go into the land, into the history of this land."[5]

The decision to plumb the depths of Norman history was major, for it would affect his writings deeply and permanently. Normandy became the locus of most of his works, while the history of the province provided subjects for several novels. His knowledge of the regional manners, customs and superstitions would come vibrantly alive in the fictional universe he was about to create. With characteristic grandeur, he conceived a cycle of historical novels with a Norman setting, to be entitled "Ouest," which never materialized, history having proven much too constricting for his unruly imagination. Instead, he wrote his first "Diabolique," "Le Dessous de cartes d'une partie de whist," which combines his love of Normandy with his lust for scandal. He shifted the scene of a work in progress, from Paris to Normandy — a felicitous decision for he thus enabled himself to complete *Une vieille maîtresse,* his first important novel. Finally, he began writing yet another major work, *L'Ensorcelée,* also set in Normandy.

Having found this ambrosial country of the mind, having found his religious, political and literary identity in the Norman past, he viewed contemporary Paris with abysmal contempt. The most thunderous attacks against what he called the "mediocracy" of the age came from his pen, supplemented by a program so outrageously reactionary that even the Legitimists could not endorse it. He argued vehemently that the Republic could not last and that only a monarchy could withstand the advance of socialism. Real progress could be made only by a return to the past, for only in the past could one find the truth and the light, symbolized by an authoritarian king who yields, if at all, to the Pope alone. Such intransigence could obviously not attract many sympathizers, and the wonder is that Barbey himself seems to have been sincere in expounding such views.

IX *First Major Works*

In 1851, he published, almost simultaneously, two seemingly contradictory works, *Les Prophètes du passé* and *Une vieille maîtresse.* The former is a series of homiletic eulogies of Joseph de Maistre, Chateaubriand, Lamennais and Blanc de Saint-Bonnet, the lay "Fathers of the Church," as he called them. The work is an expression of despair about the direction in which France was moving, and the despair is evident even in the paradoxical title, for the "prophets" exalted by Barbey belong hopelessly to another era. A contemporary critic, Francis Lacombe, summed up his impressions in this way: "Monsieur d'Aurevilly thinks like a Franciscan, while writing like a dragoon."[6] It is not an unfair appraisal.

Une vieille maîtresse represents a turning away from the stultifying limitations of Parisian milieus, back to the deeper regions of his innermost self — his Norman past. It offers yet another illustration of the mystery of passion, and by its probe into the nether world of sexual aberration and the power of carnality, is very much in the spirit of the *Diaboliques.* Innocuous when judged by twentieth-century standards, the novel was somewhat bold for the eighteen-fifties, especially coming as it did from the author of *Les Prophètes du passé.* Indignant over the alleged scandal caused by his novel and its apparent incompatibility with the views expressed in his previous work, Barbey snarled that his critics were mere bigots, seeing nothing but pettiness in their objections, and, undaunted, argued that to prohibit a Catholic writer from describing passion would be to abandon art to freethinkers. But the controversy would not abate, and Barbey later wrote two prefaces for his novel, both of them landmark documents in the history of the Catholic novel, both of them claiming to solve the unsolvable problem of art and morality.

X   *Love Again*

The year 1851 was crucial in the life of Barbey for he not only achieved a certain renown, he also met and fell in love with a young widow, Adélaide-Emilie de Sommervogel, Baronne de Bouglon. Aggressively virtuous, pious and unyielding, she was to exert a considerable influence on Barbey for several years. By his own account, he stopped drinking, resumed his religious practice and even achieved a reconciliation with his parents (after a twenty-year separation), all of this because such was the pleasure of the woman he called "L'Ange blanc." More spectacularly, he agreed to soften the tone of his writing, to repress his fascination with erotic subjects and to make his fiction more palatable to Catholic readers. The "Baronne," not unsatisfied with these dramatic changes, became his fiancée, stipulating that he must liquidate his debts before they were married. But she soon began to temporize, and the marriage never took place, though her interest in Barbey's royalties (on her son's behalf) would make her haunt Barbey down the years until the day of his death.

After Napoleon's coup, Barbey the erstwhile royalist became a fervent Bonapartist, to the dismay of some, and to the applause of his enemies. He argued that at the very least, the Emperor was against Revolution, that is, against chaos and the disintegration of society; indeed, active, forceful authority appeared to Barbey infinitely preferable to the indolence of royal pretenders: such are the arguments he developed in violent polemical articles. At the same time, he became a regular contributor to *Le Pays,* an unofficial government paper for which he wrote literary criticism. Virulent as ever, he had a stormy relationship with *Le Pays,* the expression of his own views being severely constrained by the editorial staff and as the constraints tightened like a vise he was compelled to "make tooth-picks out of oak."[7] But in spite of several breaks, he wrote for this paper until 1862; it was the first semblance of stability in a nomadic career.

XI   L'Ensorcelée

In 1855 he went cursing off to jail for refusing to serve in the National Guard, dispatching a haughty explanation to Trébutien: "The soul of old Brummell welled up within me and forbade me to touch those bourgeois horrors."[8] It is also the year when his novel *L'Ensorcelée* was first published in book form. Plot, characters, atmosphere, everything is Norman, including snatches of patois; in addition, he makes his boldest use to date of the *fantastique,* to give his characters an epic stature but also to remind us repeatedly of the supernatural — the level at which the story is most meaningful.

XII   *Baudelaire*

Frequenting literary milieus proved amply rewarding, for there he met Baudelaire and a short but significant friendship soon developed. The affinities between them went far beyond shared hatred and scorn for the ugliness and inanity of the era. Perhaps because of their common Jansenistic substratum, both were attracted by the odor of incense mixed with the odor of sin, by erotic oddities, by the idea of eternal damnation: indeed, *Les Fleurs du mal* and the *Diaboliques* were written by kindred souls. Before they met, Baudelaire had been admiring Barbey's work for some time and when he asked Barbey to borrow copies of his books which he might lend to Madame Sabatier, they quickly became friends. The poet recommended books which Barbey might consider for review, introduced him to artistic milieus and as late as 1862 he could write: "Except for D'Aurevilly, Flaubert and Sainte-Beuve, I can't get along with anybody."[9] Both were dandies, hence neither one could be (or would allow himself to be) astounded or shocked by the other. Barbey was, for Baudelaire, the "perfect monster" and Barbey addressed the poet as "Dear horror of my life." Little else is known about the relationship, but glimpses of it are nothing short of tantalizing. One evening, after Barbey stated that he was looking for a spiritual director capable of distinguishing nuances and half-tints, Baudelaire maliciously inquired: "My dear d'Aurevilly, are you claiming that you have *distinguished* twinges of remorse?"[10] Elsewhere, in his projects for the theater, Baudelaire jotted the following:

"D'Aurevily invites you to receive communion with him like someone else invites you to dinner.

'We'll receive communion together and we will kneel together, humbly, with our fists on our hips.'

'Why are you looking at those girls?'

'I will repent it."[11]

They remained close friends for several years, then drifted apart for unknown reasons.

XIII   *The Virulent Critic*

The literary criticism which Barbey published during this period is considered a bit more supple, less virulent, less provocative; the terms are quite relative, for in describing his criticism, one is always speaking of varying degrees of violence. He termed Victor Hugo's *Les Contemplations* a literary suicide. For Barbey, Hugo progressed only in the direction of absurdity and emptiness, alienation and monstrousness; and it seemed obvious to Barbey that Hugo was "dying from a hemorrhage of words without ideas." Insensitive to the power and scope of the *Contemplations,* Barbey was repelled by the apparent lack of esthetic sensitivity shown by Flaubert, "the man of marble who wrote *Madame Bovary* with a pen of stone,"[12] and although his article does not shred the fabric of Flaubert's work, it is indeed more severe than would seem warranted. Yet some of his fairest, some of his very best criticism was also written during these years. His article on Stendhal is an attempt to go beyond their obvious philosophical differences and to explain a long-standing fascination with Stendhal's work.[13] At the same time, Barbey seems to have grasped the full stature of Balzac, defending him against detractors and invoking the names of Shakespeare and Molière to situate him in literary history. Finally when Baudelaire was brought to trial for *Les Fleurs du mal,* Barbey defended the work on moral and esthetic grounds, seeing in it some of the greatness of Dante and understanding it so well that he was the first to recognize its "architecture secrète," that masterful if sometimes elusive organization of the entire work. Such, then, was Barbey's criticism: if his range of sympathies did not include Hugo and Flaubert, toward whom he appears very unfair, he is equitable, even admirable when it comes to Stendhal, Balzac and Baudelaire — no mean feat if it is borne in mind that Stendhal did not expect to be read until 1930 and that Baudelaire was prosecuted for his writings. Writing about the literature of his day with the airs of a Benvenuto Cellini, he did commit several blunders; yet he could most often probe and judge with such accuracy and foresight that his insights and judgments still remain valid over a century later.

Yet his life continued to be a melancholy succession of disappointments and false starts, even after reaching the age when most writers are well established. He took part in the founding of a newspaper, *Le Réveil,* the aim of which was to combat the literary Bohemia of the day and to give literature a Catholic orientation. Within weeks, major disagreements with his co-founders left him embittered, and within months he broke with the group. Shortly afterward, Sainte-Beuve ended his friendly relations with Barbey because of what he regarded as the latter's impertinence. As a result, Barbey was temporarily ousted from *Le Pays.* In addition, the ever-faithful Trébutien broke with Barbey for the last time, on the pretext of being horrified by Barbey's suggestion that the publication of Maurice de Guérin's works (on which the two had labored for years) be entrusted to Poulet-Malassis, the publisher of *Les Fleurs du mal* and of books judged by Trébutien to be pornographic. Barbey soon suffered the ignominy of seeing de Guérin published with a preface by his newest enemy, Sainte-Beuve. The list of reversals goes on, however, for Mme de Bouglon again postponed their projected marriage. He consoled himself as best he could from these misfortunes by resuming his creation of a fictional world and by lampooning the world in which he was forced to live.

Within the entire range of his Napoleonic activity, *Les Quarante Médaillons de l'Académie* ("The Forty Medallions of the Academy") represents hardly a minor skirmish, yet these acid portraits of members of the French Academy brought about a government decree compelling *Le Nain Jaune*, the newspaper in which they appeared, to cease publication. Unruffled, Barbey published his *Médaillons* in book form in 1864, as much a pronunciamento of his critical views as it is a vitriolic attack against the hollow pomp and pretense of officialdom in the arts and sciences.

XIV   Le Chevalier des Touches

By 1865, he had returned to *Le Pays* and left again, exacerbated over having been a pawn in the grotesque chess-game played between a heavy-handed government censor and the paper's editorial staff. Fortunately the *Nain Jaune,* resurrected and transformed, had not kept a grudge, so Barbey was accepted again, and began to write denunciations of the government. By this time, he was arousing less hostility, for while his colleagues might ridicule the outmoded ruffles of the dandy's attire, they did respect his vigor and his integrity. Furthermore, they shared his hostility toward the state of affairs in France during the 1860's and his need for violent protest against an all-pervasive stupidity.

The *Nain Jaune* also published a lengthy novel of his, *Le Chevalier des Touches,* re-published in book form in 1864. Somewhat in the spirit of Scott's *Chronicles of the Canongate* (indeed he wanted to be the Walter Scott of Normandy), it is intended to be a historical novel, its subject being an episode from the guerrilla warfare waged by the Chouans. However, the demands of the author's imagination kept asserting themselves so that the result is unreliable history but colorful and dramatic fiction. Jules Vallès, several light-years away from Barbey in political thought, was one of the first to praise the novel, which was widely read because it contained nothing objectionable to faith or morals.

XV Un Prêtre marié

Such was not the case, however, with *Un Prêtre marié* ("A Married Priest"), published in 1865, a novel which had the curious effects of drawing a shrill condemnation from Zola and of being anathematized by the Archbishop of Paris. It is based on "the great Christian idea of Expiation,"[14] an idea which had long interested Barbey ever since he had first read about it in Joseph de Maistre. But the book also bears the unmistakable influence of Byron's satanism and the conflict of the two opposing forces of infinite good and infinite evil creates an atmosphere reminiscent of a medieval morality play, with the author considerably more fascinated by his Satan-figure than might have been expected. Léon Bloy was one of the first to appreciate the novel fully, but his laudatory article did not appear until 1876. In 1874, however, *Un Prêtre marié* was one of the few contemporary works to win the praise of J.-K. Huysmans' hero, Des Esseintes, in *A Rebours (Against the Grain)*.

XVI *The Exasperated Critic*

In spite of this productivity, the eighteen-sixties were remarkably gloomy, even in the context of Barbey's generally mirthless life. The recognition he so ardently sought had not yet come, the old *ennui* returned, alternating with the sadness and rancor he felt over his losses and failures in love and friendship as well as in politics and literature. Dissipation protected him against excessive solitude, and he derived a vague sense of purpose from his continuing castigation of his times. In another series of short articles, "Les Trente-sept Médaillonnets du Parnasse contemporain," ("The Thirty-Seven 'Medallionets' of the Contemporary Parnassus"), he unleashed his repressed anger, inveighing against one of his favorite targets, a literary coterie, in this case the Parnassian poets. He saw in them nothing but pallid imitators, unfeeling and unthinking monomaniacs of metrical pyrotechnics; he was especially ruthless toward Mallarmé, whose poetry always remained one of his more regrettable blind-spots.

Wherever he looked, he began seething, and while he painstakingly wrote his masterpiece, the *Diaboliques,* during the decade of 1863-73, he went on expressing his increasingly passionate hatred of the nineteenth century in the pages of the *Nain Jaune.* These essays in social criticism, later published in a volume entitled *Les Ridicules du temps,* bring to mind the condemnations hurled at the century by Jules Vallès in *Les Réfractaires* and *La Rue,* or again by Louis Veuillot in *Les Odeurs de Paris.* More than ever, Barbey found real *grandeur* only in the past, for the philistines were everywhere and literature had sunk to sub-cultural depths. Even the vices were petty so that only the ludicrous, in its infinite variations, was worthy of attention; priests were spineless, France was plagued by blue-stockings, and the world was governed by eunuchs.

Obviously, few editors would dare welcome such a raging iconoclast, so he faced still more lean years. Financial need compelled him to write theater criticism, even though he had already expressed — in print — his dislike for contemporary theater. He viewed the drama as a more limited genre than the novel because it does not have analysis and description at its disposal. Too immediate, it does not allow for reflection; it appeals to the lower instincts of the mob. Moreover, the props, the setting, the actor's voice, the beauty of an actress, and all the other externals are mere distractions, devices for concealing mediocrity. In short, for Barbey the aristocrat and the intellectual, theater was vulgar. His biases were confirmed when he became a regular theater-goer and discovered that the "giants" of the day were Emile Augier, Alexandre Dumas fils and Victorien Sardou and that the theater was shot through with "scribisme," that mania for the contrived which betrays no preoccupation with the depths of the human heart.

In 1869, upon the death of Sainte-Beuve, Barbey replaced him as a regular contributor to *Le Constitutionnel,* a position he kept (with brief interruptions) until his own death in 1889. But there is something hollow about this achievement, since the prestige of this newspaper had been slowly declining. When the War broke out in 1870, Barbey joined the National Guard with no illusions whatever: had he not prophesied the Apocalypse? Dejected, he left for Normandy shortly after the Prussian siege of Paris and before the eruption of the "Commune," but for the moment, Normandy offered no tranquility, since he had to settle the complicated business of his father's estate. When the debts were finally paid off, there was little money left and no property: "We were born to be rich; all we have left is the piece of bread which gives pride its independence."[15] Feeling uprooted by the loss of his property, he left Saint-Sauveur (his native village) for Valognes, the little town where he had first known love, and which he was about to immortalize in his *Diaboliques.*

His vanity was flattered, however, when, in February 1872, certain Parisian newspapers began speculating that his prolonged absence was simply due to his having married a rich heiress! He returned to Paris, promising himself that he would leave again soon, to haunt his Norman past, but his literary situation having improved, he postponed his departure. He became a chronicler for *Le Figaro* and, for once in his life, was pleased with the financial arrangements. He also contributed to *Le Gaulois* and to *Le Constitutionnel.* His novels began to be republished; and Palmé pursued the publication of his collected critical writings, *Les Oeuvres et les Hommes,* a series which eventually comprised some twenty-five volumes. Finally, when Dentu agreed to bring out *Les Diaboliques,* Barbey enjoyed the most rewarding situation of his life. It would not last, however, beyond 1874.

Not finding much to comment on in the new literature of the early seventies, he studied the political situation and wrote polemical articles, vociferating in favor of moral "law and order" and decrying the general imbecility of contemporary France. He still advocated the restoration of absolute monarchy and professed his scorn for politics and for all political figures including the pretender to the French throne, but he was obviously fascinated by the whole mad spectacle. In 1872 he also wrote art criticism for *Le Gaulois.* Granted, he lacked the time to document himself properly, and he knew precious little about artistic technique; but the function of the critic, he argued, was to express the emotion inspired by the work — a second-rate emotion, to be sure, for he had long ago stated his unequivocal position toward art when he wrote that he would "give all the cathedrals in the world in exchange for a tress of Diane de Poitiers" (II, 743).

His circle of friends began to broaden, as he reconciled differences with some of his contemporaries, including writers whose works he had once judged severely: François Coppée, Edmond de Goncourt, Théodore de Banville. As for Zola, Barbey remained adamant, publishing a scathing article on *Le Ventre de Paris,* taking Zola to task for his myopic materialism and for the stupefying vulgarity of his subject. No, with Zola there would never be even the beginning of understanding. Barbey greatly preferred

Léon Cladel, that frenzied republican whose rural "portraits" glowed with color and feeling — Cladel, a man needful of lessons in political theory, but in literature a veritable Rubens. Another "devil in an inkwell," much younger, stridently Catholic, Léon Bloy became Barbey's factotum; when proofs came in from the printer, Bloy was the Minister in charge of corrections, especially if the Master was away from Paris. From Valognes where he liked to spend time with the ghosts of his youth, Barbey dispatched messages post-haste — anxious, urgent messages which endowed spelling and punctuation with all the importance of the affairs of state.[16]

During the years immediately preceding the publication of the *Diaboliques,* he also turned out a long series of articles on Goethe and Diderot.[17] The latter had long been one of his "intellectual vices"; instinctively, he had been drawn to Diderot's fiery nature, his tempestuous imagination, the intense vivaciousness of his style, but could never justify writing about him at any length, because of Diderot's religious and political views. Professor Jacques Petit's explanation is, here again, quite convincing: "In fact, his reaction to Diderot reveals the paradox which lies at the very center of his criticism: it wants to be dogmatic and remains most often tied to his impressions."[18] No such paradox existed, however, in the case of Goethe, for Barbey had never understood anyone's enthusiasm for the German sage — hence his criticism is an exercise in debunking, and its central theme is the impassivity of Goethe — that man of marble — contrasted with Diderot, the man of fire.

XVII   Les Diaboliques

From Valognes, on December 16, 1874, Barbey frantically wrote his publisher, Dentu, informing him that he was leaving for Paris immediately, adding: "If we haven't avoided the seizure, let us at least try to avoid the trial. Let us combine all our efforts and if you must act before my arrival, act toward that end."[19] Alarmed by malicious book-reviewers, the public prosecutor's office had ordered the sale of the *Diaboliques* stopped, the unsold copies (some 480, out of a total of 2,200 printed) had been impounded, and a judicial inquiry had been opened. Horrified at the thought of appearing in court, Barbey mobilized all the friends and acquaintances who might be useful, obtaining even the intervention of

Léon Gambetta, the Radical leader and future Premier. After considerable maneuvering, Barbey and his friends succeeded in having the charges dismissed, with the stipulation that the impounded copies of the book be destroyed.

More than any other work, *Les Diaboliques* secured a solid niche for its author in French literary history. It is a collection of six lengthy short stories: "Le rideau cramoisi" ("The Crimson Curtain"), "Le plus bel amour de Don Juan" ("Don Juan's Finest Love"), "Le bonheur dans le crime" ("Happiness in Crime"), "Le dessous de cartes d'une partie de whist" ("The Under-side of the Cards"), "A un dîner d'athées" ("At a Dinner of Atheists"), and "La vengeance d'une femme" ("A Woman's Vengeance"). No one, to date, has discovered any "secret architecture" in the arrangement of the stories, though all of them share a poetry of evil, constituted in large part by the raptures of lust and the haunting, almost hallucinatory quality of passion seen as the ultimate reality, even as a supra-reality. *Les Diaboliques* is indeed his masterpiece, containing, as it does, the quintessence of his genius as a story-teller; his skillful use of the tale told within a tale, his ability to lead up, artfully, to a shocking ending, his genius for re-creating the Norman setting and for evoking the eerie workings of passion: it is all there, much of it hopelessly remote, no doubt, from late twentieth-century readers, but the work resurrects this distant past and endows it with the intense vibrancy of life. His contemporaries viewed the matter differently, however, playing up the apparent incompatibility between the work and the author's outspoken Catholicism.

XVIII   *The Norman Dandy*

Embittered by a controversy he could have predicted, even if he had considered only the large number and the bad faith of his enemies, wearied by further disagreements with newspaper editors, he returned to Normandy, as he would do almost every autumn, with the great September tides. The reasons for these constant returns are sentimental, for he had grown to love dearly the region which had so well served his literary needs. He went "home" often, in order to live with his "spectres," the ghosts of his youth and the shadows of a more distant past, but "younger" ones too — creatures to whom he himself had given life: des Touches, or the be-

witched woman, or the married priest. No, in Normandy, he was
never alone: "... all the souls *I have known there* crowd in, gather-
ing around me, and thus the invisible fills the visible for me and
gives a bitter charm to the eternal landscape which does not die and
has not changed one iota since my youth."[20] It pleased him to be
the gentleman-in-residence, one of the last members of a dying spe-
cies, and he took up "headquarters" at the splendid Hôtel de
Grandval-Caligny in Valognes. The local population deferred to
him, for he had written about them and their ancestors in books —
published in Paris! To these people he was "Môssieu Jeule" (as he
liked to repeat, imitating their heavy Norman accent), the scion of
a well-known if impoverished family. With them, the cult of the
past seemed less anachronistic, and old customs were still alive:
politeness, for instance, that vanishing art of keeping a man at a
distance, or alms-giving, outside church after Sunday mass.

Still, financial necessity would not allow him to retire completely, so he spent three seasons out of four in Paris, compensating
for the ghastliness of the century by hating it passionately — in all
its pomps and all its works: democracy ("the sovereignty of
wretchedness"), and other vulgarities such as tolerance, pluralism,
secular education and universal suffrage. He protested against all
of it, in his writings, of course, but also in the style of his clothing,
affecting braid, lace and color which contrasted sharply with the
black plainness then in vogue. He also dyed his hair, used perfume,
and covered his improbable persona with the cape of a Norman
carter, an enormous, sweeping white cape with broad stripes
(reddish, blue or brown) and lined with silk or velvet. Such is how
he would stroll down the Paris boulevards, with the bearing of a
cavalry officer, and those who saw him would remember too the
pirate's profile and the musketeer mustache.

This haughtiness is intensified in his critical writings, as the circle
of his hatreds widened. He broke with the Catholic milieus, partly
because they were so prudish and partly, too, one suspects, because
Catholicism has ceased to be that high balcony from which one
could spit on the mob.[21] Then, in 1877, he published *Les Bas-bleus,*
a violent attack on bluestockings, the expression of a hatred conceived long ago and legitimized for Barbey by Joseph de Maistre
who had proclaimed, "When woman wants to emulate man, she
becomes a monkey."[22] The work merely placed another barrier between Barbey and his enemies who preferred not to notice that his

real targets are the pretentiousness and pedantry of certain woman-writers and that an author lacking those faults (Madame de Staël, for one, whom he truly respected) came off generally unscathed. Writing drama criticism again, he conceded that the Naturalist theater might well be an innovation, but it still remained a mud-bath, while traditional drama was for him the embodiment of dull-ness itself. Could one expect anything else, considering that nineteenth-century thought was "sinking, disappearing in the abyss of madness and the frenzied desire for annihilation"?[23]

XIX *Last Years*

To the very end of his life, Barbey d'Aurevilly remained prodi-giously active, devoting his final years chiefly to the publication of his collected critical works (*Les Oeuvres et les Hommes*), to the preparation of new editions of his novels, to the writing of one final novel, *Une histoire sans nom (A Story without a Name),* not to mention miscellaneous writings. In addition, he was "lionized" by a group of young writers.

Une histoire sans nom proved to be his most commercially suc-cessful novel, for by 1882 (the year of its publication) he had achieved some of the renown so vehemently sought after for half a century: he had indeed become "a name." It is also one of his bleakest and most sinister works, expressing the irrevocable nature of human solitude, combining Gothic elements with a denunciation of Jansenism and, once again, religion with eroticism.

Une page d'histoire, also published in 1882, is more an evoca-tion, a reverie, than a short story. It shows the author, haunted by the theme of incest, conjuring up the memory of a young and charming couple, Marguerite and Julien de Ravalet de Tourlaville, executed for incest in 1603. That his sympathies lie with the "crimi-nals, the text makes abundantly clear.

The following year he published *Ce qui ne meurt pas (What Never Dies),* a lengthy novel written in his youth, portraying passion as an absolute, passion as a destructive force, passion as the one truly fascinating object of study for Barbey.

Better understood than ever before, at least by an elite, he had earned the respect and friendship of writers too numerous to list here. At the home of José-Maria de Hérédia or of François Coppée, he met other writers; he became close friends with Théodore de Banville, and Edmond de Goncourt selected him to become a member of his newly founded Académie. Frequently hosted by Alphonse Daudet, he opened his doors for his "Dimanches," at first to a chosen few, hand-picked by Léon Bloy, then to a larger group, some of whom went out of curiosity, others out of admiration; but all those who did go came away with respect. He was, however, much more than a hospitable, venerated writer, thriving on well-merited adulation. He wrote enthusiastic articles on these younger men, — Maurice Rollinat, whom he considered a musician in verse, or again Jean Richepin, whose sacrilegious anger made him shudder. For Léon Bloy, he was a mentor in both literary and religious matters, and Bloy would be one of his few real disciples. Another was Jean Lorrain whose novel, *Monsieur de Bougrelon,* is a first-rate caricature of Barbey and a pastiche of his literary manner.

He died on April 23, 1889.

CHAPTER 2

Dandyism: Theoretical and Practical

I *Origin and Evolution*

T HE concept of dandyism continues to be misconstrued, despite
a long lineage of dandies in French literature, from Balzac to
Proust and despite a goodly number of scholarly works on the subject.[1] Its origin is to be found in the London of the seventeen-
nineties, where its vogue and cult were established by George Bryan
Brummell, king of the snobs, high priest of taste and fashion,
whose career as "arbiter elegantiae" spanned the years 1795-1816.
Unspeakably phlegmatic, he was perhaps the only thoroughgoing
dandy in history, an admixture of vanity, polite scorn and insolence
pushed beyond cynicism to the point of attaining imagination and
art. Bewitching his admirers with his indifference to others and his
narcissistic cult of self, he rehabilitated snobbery by boasting about
his own, and developed a conscious, deliberate, outrageous snobbery which added to his seductiveness. Hence, when he appeared in
a bored and snobbish London wearing a starched cravat folded
with prodigious precision, affecting an air of prideful disdain and
willful coldness, dandyism became virtually inevitable.

Some of the misunderstanding about dandyism can be dispelled
by emphasizing that it encompasses far more than externals, for it
is in essence an art of living, of facing oneself and others, of imposing one's own arbitrary order on the chaos of life. It is a framework
broad enough to allow for personal innovation, a framework
within which the self can become a work of art. Prodigious self-
discipline is required, a restraint not usually found in the man of
the world; for the dandy must avoid any betrayal of his feelings, he
must suppress all desire — and the expression of interest in anything or anyone is beneath his lofty dignity. If perchance an emo-

41

tion is felt, all the resources of the soul must be mobilized to ensure that it will not show, since nothing is more ridiculous than spontaneity. While systematized snobbery is an integral part of dandyism, so too are the art and science of appearance. The affectation of granting undue consideration to all the forms of one's appearance or to what others would dismiss as trivia is counterbalanced by the affecting of total indifference when performing an action viewed by others as important. The dandy acts as if the self were of tremendous import and spends his day doing nothing of any apparent consequence; indeed, to do nothing, but to do it methodically — while looking bored — is a dandy's occupation. It is within such a context that externals, such as dress, language and behavior acquire a meaning not inherent in them by nature.

Dandyism is a British eccentricity brought to France when the émigrés of the Revolution returned from exile. The existence of the dandy in the Paris of the eighteen-thirties is amply attested to by the all-seeing Balzac; Henri de Marsay in *La Fille aux yeux d'or,* Lucien de Rubempré in *Illusions perdues* (and in *Splendeurs et misères des courtisanes*) exemplify the type at least as well as Prince Korasov in Stendhal's *Le Rouge et le Noir* and Julien Sorel himself has a trace of the dandy about him. Ardent Anglomaniacs, the French Romantics appropriated dandyism, but transformed it, using it in part to combat their avowed enemy, the bourgeois. It must be remembered here that by the eighteen-thirties the doleful Romanticism of Lamartine had been replaced by a flamboyant, passionate kind, strongly marked by the influence of satanism and Byronism.

Dandyism was adapted to the French temperament, and Paris saw many a fashionable young man combining elegance with Latin effervescence: noisy, rude, his apparent "raison d'être" being to attract attention to his foppish person, trying to pass for a sportsman by going to the races and, with seeming competence, discoursing on steeplechase, handicaps or some other aspect of horsemanship. Soon the dandy was known for his frivolousness and profligacy and one of the final avatars was the "lion." Firm distinctions are difficult to establish, especially since, in the literature of the time, the terms "dandy" and "lion" are often used interchangeably; but it is generally agreed that by the end of the decade, the latter was the more elegant and fashionable of the two. Master of the boulevards, he had the arrogance of a conquistador and boundless contempt for the beliefs and passions of everyman. Scornful of traditional "galanterie," he was a cynical Don Juan who treated women with haughty insolence and delighted in blowing cigar-smoke in their faces. Obnoxious with his braggadocio, he never removed his spurs — except to go to bed or to ride a horse.

II *Barbey's Dandyism*

Many of the nuances of Parisian dandyism are found in Barbey at his début in 1836 and during the years of his apprenticeship: the elegance, the merciless irony, the snobbery, and that look of insufferable boredom. He loved the standoffishness, the impertinent apartness, the aristocratic reserve which it required. Starting out as a "conventional" dandy, he eventually moved toward a more personal and philosophical version. His personal journal (*Memoranda*) for the years 1836-1839 is replete with notations about his dress, his lengthy preparations for going out; his tailor is as important as his coiffeur and the coming of either one is treated with the solemnity of a state visit. Obsessed with his appearance, he can sometimes see the vapidity of this obsession and turn his irony against himself, but most often he remains extremely serious. When finally after hours of preparation, he does manage to attend a soirée, his pleasures often consist of breaking his Olympian silence with an occasional epigram or indulging in some other form of sarcasm. Almost daily, he records his visits to fashionable cafés and restaurants, ritualistic visits performed without enthusiasm, simply because being a dandy requires one's presence at Tortoni's or the Jockey Club at a specified time. Occasionally, the entry is a bit more spirited, as when he refers to the "Café Anglais, that Sodom, where dancers, singers, gamblers, military types, journalists — the whole Sanhedrin of the devil — were drinking, smoking, yelling and rather promiscuously annoying one another" (II, 844).

But it would be unfair to imply that he remained a complete slave of dandyism. His financial limitations, his savage nature, and his need for solitude prevented him from becoming so subservient as to sacrifice his individuality to a lifestyle for which he was only partly suited. Further, his patrician manners, his aristocratic tastes, and his English air combined with the name "d'Aurevilly," were welcomed in certain salons of the posh Faubourg Saint-Germain, where his appreciation for traditional courtesy also found its place. Dandyism for Barbey meant sustained constraint and ongoing conflict; though he remained obsessed by the image of Brummell and though he strove to preserve an icy elegance or at least the dandy's impassiveness, his impetuous nature often won out: the roar of the "lion" could not always be suppressed. Until the very end of his life, he practiced the kind of dandyism which prefers provocative brashness to deadly indifference.

III   Dandyism and Love

A.   La Bague d'Annibal

Written in 1834, when the influence of Byron's cynicism had reached its peak, *La Bague d'Annibal* treats love as conflict: the conflict between prideful self-domination and the humiliation of surrender. The setting too contributes to the conflict, since the protagonists belong to the elegant and mindless society of Parisian *salons,* a world in which boredom leads to meanness and conversations consist in destroying reputations — a true hot-house of artificiality, where the mortal sin lies in being human, i.e. loving, passionate, sincere.

Joséphine d'Alcy, one of the main characters, discovers one day that she has two suitors. Baudouin d'Artinel is an eminently stale, respectable, unctuous judge, wily and Machiavellian, who speaks with dubious tenderness to Joséphine about his deceased wife, in order to win Joséphine's affection. But Mme d'Alcy, presumably a widow, seems absorbed, even lost, in her conversations with Aloys de Synarose, a young, flamboyant dandy, determined to leave his true feelings shrouded in mystery. In the end, Baudouin wins, marrying Joséphine who prefers sentimentality to passion and the security of Baudouin to the inscrutable nature of Aloys.

Mme d'Alcy represents Barbey's first attempt to give a female character some degree of complexity, and yet she is but a shadow when compared to later heroines, notably that astounding group of creations called the "Diaboliques." Characteristically enough, Barbey repeatedly underscores the enigmatic quality of Joséphine: Sphinx-like, "her memories were hieroglyphics" (I, 143), and the mysterious element in her moves the narrator to add that Talleyrand himself would have been easier to decipher (I, 144). Such re-

marks reveal Barbey's inability — or unwillingness — to probe
deeply into the female psyche, and also his obsession with the eternal feminine mystery, But this mystery in no way attenuates
Barbey's misogyny; extremely harsh toward Joséphine, he seizes
every opportunity to denigrate her, reminding us often of her
vapidity, referring to her as a woman "who was always thinking
... about looking as if she were thinking" (I, 179). Or again he
writes, in reference to her *thoughts:* "if one can apply that ambitious term to the frail product of Mme d'Alcy's gaseous brain"
(I, 164).

Hence, the reader wonders what draws Aloys to such a feature-
less woman: perhaps the mystery about her? Or perhaps like Barbey he has a penchant for women in their autumn years, women
who, like Joséphine, have skin resembling "slightly yellowed
ivory" and "sick, exhausted lips" (I, 142) — all of this despite her
tender age of twenty-seven. But the question is never answered:
often in Barbey's fictional world, love simply exists, without psychological justification, and that in itself constitutes a statement
about love. One does not doubt, however, the extent of Aloys'
love, or the fierceness of his struggle to keep this love concealed
both from its object and from society.

The nature of this society has been hinted at above, but its
importance for an understanding of Aloys cannot be overemphasized. It is described as an "advanced" society, yet apart from
excessive sophistication and phoniness, its advanced age has merely
brought intolerable boredom. Relief from this boredom is sought
in the most malicious and cruel kind of gossip, in slander or in
scandal-mongering. Aware that they are being watched by vultures,
Joséphine and Aloys must not betray their secret. While both are
equally sensitive to the possibility of being verbally flayed and
strangled by their acquaintances, Aloys seems the more determined
of the two that he will not become their victim. He, more intensely
than Joséphine, barricades himself in his interior fortress, using his
gift of language to fire off virulent epigrams, "shooting snipe with
high-caliber bullets" (I, 160) thereby amusing and distracting his
listeners.

The war is waged on other fronts as well, a war dictated by pride
and Aloys' concern with his self-image. Bearing a close resemblance to Barbey, Aloys remains perpetually enraptured with himself and with his image. He belongs to an elite with an ego "bigger

than the world" (I,166), an elite which considers woman either as a
succubus, a cushion, or a pleasure-machine. This elite, this group
of "superior" beings, though vulnerable to women's "steel
piercer" (I, 167) does not die from such wounds. The very vocabulary employed here points up one of Barbey's favorite equations:
that of love and suffering, a suffering which feeds on itself, grows,
and is inflicted on the person who threatens to tear the mask from
the dandy's face. Love then, directed by pride, becomes quite the
opposite of communication; it signifies increased isolation, self-
imposed suffering, entrenchment within the self and psychological
arteriosclerosis. The author excels in describing the various phases
of this progression.

For although Aloys is madly in love, his disclaimers — to
"friends" and acquaintances — are multiplied: the mask gets
thicker as his love increases. Moved by pride to crush her vanity
like glass (I, 171), he himself is broken by his resolution, as shown
by a sudden attack of gastritis, pneumonia and inflammation of the
brain, which amounts to an accurate portrait of the dandy in love:
a steaming cauldron beneath layers of ice. After a brief respite,
Aloys returns to and maintains this aloofness, this stony muteness
which Joséphine must suffer. Indeed, not a word escapes him
about his true feelings; and we witness his deliberate coldness, his
impassivity, his vicious refusal to betray any positive feeling. In
response, Joséphine experiences to the full the only feeling of which
her vanity has left her capable — an acrid, burning curiosity, a
craving to flatter her ego by discovering signs that he is enraptured
with her. To this end she first plays the role of coquette with her
other suitor, Baudouin, and later she virtually offers herself to
Aloys on the one occasion when he sees her alone. On this fateful
evening, the events of which will determine the outcome of the
story, Aloys, we are told, expends ten years of his life in repressing
his desire for her. He leaves, bursting with self-satisfaction at
having replied "Madame" when she addressed him by his first
name, thereby maintaining his distance, thereby too keeping his
mask in place.

Mention should also be made of the Spanish balcony scene witnessed by the narrator shortly before the marriage. Late one night
Baudouin is seen climbing to the balcony of Joséphine's apartment
where the latter, unclad, greets him as he enters, closing the door
behind him. The narrator, however, does not share this knowledge

with his "friends" in the *salons* which he frequents, and thus hypocrisy triumphs on all fronts: the narrator, in not sharing his knowledge with the social clan (which he should do to prove his loyalty to the code of indiscriminate slander) becomes the accomplice of Baudouin and Joséphine, whose secret love affair will be kept from the "vultures"; and Aloys, during the wedding ceremony, keeps a perfect composure, never once betraying his true feelings for Joséphine. He even gives proof of his cleverness and presence of mind by reminding the narrator of Hannibal's ring, employing this symbol to express a peculiar personal conviction: the wedding ring, like the ring containing poison used by Hannibal to commit suicide, contains a subtle poison which kills, not a person, but love. The narrator extends the meaning of the symbol by stating that we all have such rings in our lives, rings worn by women we loved who married someone else.

La Bague d'Annibal remains a literary curio, a fascinating period piece, a story about "pastel colored vengeance" as the author wrote (I, 1271). Yet despite its positive elements, the story is alightly marred by exacerbated irony which at times becomes excessive; one regrets that the author went to school to Byron and learned so thoroughly the lesson of that great cynic.

B. L'Amour impossible

The novel on which Barbey worked intermittently from 1837 to 1840 brings us back into the world of *La Bague d'Annibal,* that world in which cynical aristocrats move about, magnificent and bored, and where Parisian begums and beys thrive on vicious slander in elegant drawing-rooms or in boudoirs of jonquil-colored satin. The story's title deftly sums up its theme and the author has unquestionably succeeded in achieving his declared purpose: "to show love in souls grown old, lack of rapture, frigidity and at the same time a sovereign, poisoned passion, doubtless the agony of the ability to love, but an eternal agony" (I, 1246). For this particular story, the memory of his liaison with the Marquise du Vallon might have sufficed; but Barbey had read Stendhal's *Armance,* one of the first major novels on impotence, and one feels the chill of Stendhalian irony throughout *L'Amour impossible.*

The setting is the chic Faubourg Saint-Germain in the Paris of the Restoration. The "hero" is Raimbaud de Maulévrier, a dandy, and therefore a man who must at all cost dominate his own feelings and subordinate those of anyone he encounters; he must conquer without seeming to want to and must of course never be conquered. In order to dazzle his fellow-snobs, Raimbaud decides that the Marquise Bérangère de Gesvres will be his mistress, but he soon finds himself hopelessly in love with her. Mme de Gesvres, the very embodiment of nineteenth-century boredom and cynicism, hopes that an emotional involvement might alleviate the tedium of her existence; but she quickly discovers the futility of her efforts and her hope, for she has lost forever the ability to love. Her emotional impotence is communicated to Raimbaud, but they remain deeply attached to one another in a curious, non-sexual way. The real victim of this tragedy in a boudoir is Caroline d'Anglure, who dies from grief after realizing that she has lost Raimbaud, her former lover.

The sub-title of the work is "Chronique parisienne'" and although *La Bague d'Annibal* has already introduced us to this particular social world — that of a highly refined, "advanced" society, witty, skeptical and mildly sadistic, it is depicted rather more fully here, both in itself and in its nefarious effects upon the main characters. Its cult of refinement and elegance is obsessive, overpowering, and its dictates are forceful: the great sin against elegance is to place one's personal impressions or feelings above prevailing customs; personal feelings should be suppressed and sincerity is met with derision. The norm requires the substitution of pride, artifice and dissimulation for authenticity, and "grace consists in playing with what is most serious in one's feelings and thoughts" (I, 72). As for love, society's teachings are equally indisputable: love does not exist, and that which an individual misconstrues as love is a debasement; for it means a capitulation, the ugly yielding of oneself to another. In addition, sexual roles have been reversed, since woman has replaced man as a conqueror; and Barbey notes this development with the powerless anger of a castrated male (I, 62).

To the extent that she illustrates the dessication brought about by the subservience of the heart to the mind and the willingness to sacrifice truth to appearances, Bérangère de Gesvres is representative of her society, which does not mean that she cannot be distinguished from it: "Woman without unity, as strange as the Chimera of antiquity, Proteus, chameleon, the devil incarnate, she was perhaps the greatest tormentor of souls to have ever existed. Not exactly a man, she wasn't quite a woman either" (I, 118). This "empress of beauty" (I, 47) who thus combines qualities of the Sphinx and those of the hermaphrodite is also the domineering type of woman with which Barbey was obsessed all his life, the *femme fatale* with cold, piercing, virile eyes, "the eyes of a statesman of genius" (I, 46). She also has the strong will of a statesman, an iron will utilized to project a certain image of herself, a façade intended chiefly to conceal the depths of her ennui. Her ennui is abysmal, exceeding by far the level tolerated by society. It is congenital, it is her most basic feeling and must constantly be kept in check. In order to divert attention from her ennui, she preaches libertinism, repeating that one must do whatever one finds amusing; but if her argument had been turned against her, she would have asked rhetorically whether she had ever stated that *she* had found anything amusing (I, 51). "Thus, she had the language of corruption but she was not corrupt . . ." (*ibid.*).

Although she has succeeded in keeping her ennui well dissimulated, she must still contend with this ennui; and she hopes that passion might give her life a sense of purpose, unaware of the many obstacles which lie in the path of her passion. She is, after all, very much a product of that society which sees passion as self-debasement, a society in which integrity, if it means anything at all, means pride and complete self-possession. Then too there are obstacles of a more general order: the neurotic compulsion to protect herself against possible hurt and equally important, her conception of love. "She developed a thesis of transcendental love. She made it prodigious, African, chimerical; clearly beyond everything which is known and done in Paris; arguing boldly that whatever was not that exclusive love, all-absorbing, immense, did not deserve to be called love" (I, 69). At the same time, she agrees that if she were to achieve this kind of love, she would jeer at it. By the end of the nineteenth century, such attitudes will have become quite familiar: the thirst for the impossible allied with a preconception of reality. For Bérangère de Gesvres, the result of this attitude will be an inability to love, a "sad life, a feeling without a name, a relationship which society did not understand" (I, 132). This condition comes about despite her attempts to whip up passionate feelings even by means of jealousy.

Thoroughly blasée, she can be shaken out of her torpor only by the spectacle of suffering; hence, Raimbaud becomes more

"interesting" to her in direct proportion to the degree of his suffering (I, 106). And when he informs her that his recent mistress,
Caroline d'Anglure, has finally realized that she is losing him, Mme
de Gesvres reacts in the following manner: "'Oh! tell me about it!'
she said, writhing in her lounge chair, in her pink muslin peignoir,
breathing deeply from a delightful engraved flask she was holding.
'Speak, my friend,' she repeated with incredible sensuousness. And
the near-lascivious movement of the small of her back was reminiscent of Leda awaiting her swan and preparing herself for pleasure"
(I, 104). Later in Barbey's works, this association of pleasure and
inflicted pain will be much more intense and deeply felt, for it is an
integral part of his world-view.

   Raimbaud de Maulévrier, a Parisian dandy, an "effeminate Sardanapalus," has much in common with Bérangère de Gesvres. He
possesses that same lack of spontaneity, that same control exercised
by the will over the most authentic impulses of the heart, but to a
lesser degree. When the novel opens, Raimbaud has already "debased himself" because of his well-known liaison with Caroline
d'Anglure, and as the story progresses he falls passionately in love
with Bérangère. His social moorings too are somewhat more flexible than hers: though he belongs to this same society, he does
maintain a sense of perspective, a certain detachment, for he has
observed it closely and found it wanting. Lacking the strength to
reject it outright — or to risk being rejected by it — he needs this
social world if only as something against which to rebel privately,
and thus he can savor the pleasures of a double life. Outwardly
loyal to the social code of decorous ennui and cynicism, he becomes
ever more passionately and quite uncynically involved with Bérangère. In this ambivalent attitude toward society, we find a variation
on a theme which is central to Barbey's fictional universe. Although Raimbaud has grown indifferent in religious matters, he
has kept a nostalgia for sin, and the social laws forbidding passion
serve a function analogous to the equivalent religious laws; a *social*
Jansenism has been substituted for religious rigorism and through
the pursuit of passion, the pleasure of transgression remains intact.

   This pleasure pales, however, when viewed in the light of that
which love reveals about an individual. Such is the self-torture
involved in this particular love that it becomes tinged with masochism; for Raimbaud must, like the knight in the days of courtly
love, exert super-human efforts merely to prove to Bérangère the

sincerity of his love. Yet, when he ultimately succeeds, he earns, not her love, but simply her esteem. In this process of persuasion, love is shown to be a depraving force, a source of degradation and cruelty, all of which is made quite explicit in the narrator's observation that "there are moments in life when, in order to kiss the hem of a skirt, you would walk over the body of a woman whom just yesterday you adored with such idolatry" (I, 74).

To be trampled by Maulévrier is the fate of Caroline d'Anglure, the very opposite of Bérangère, a woman whose sincerity and total dedication to her lover are beyond doubt. She has the fresh, ethereal beauty of spring; and for a moment she appears to be hopelessly conventional, commonplace, and dull. In the Parisian salons, however, she is the exception, and therefore holds considerable interest: ". . . all her alabaster fragility . . . all her infinite daintiness ["delicatesses"] . . . made of Mme d'Anglure a delicacy much sought after by the intellectual sybarites of modern love" (I, 59). Strongly attracted to Raimbaud, she pursues her heart's desire — thereby acting as a free agent in an unfree society — and she gives herself completely to him, exposing herself to "all the dangers of happiness" (I, 96). Unmindful that her beauty is highly ephemeral, hence doomed, she precipitates the death of passion and her own death by not withholding at least part of her total gift of self. So abundant and graphic are the details indicating her rapid deterioration that one suspects the author of "delectatio morosa" which might be seen too in his ruthless insistence on her fragile nature and her inept choice of a lover, or again in his description of female cruelty: ". . . those pretty creatures, half bee and half viper who, concerning the Countess, never forgot to put a bit of venom in their honey" (I, 97). Such vivid imagery, anticipating Baudelaire, could well apply to most women in Barbey's fictional universe, while also illustrating one of society's chief functions (reminiscent of the chorus in Greek tragedies), namely to echoe life's all-pervasive cruelty. Thus, after the Countess' death, society does not hesitate to accuse Madame de Gesvres of having killed her. Strange, sadistic oratorio in which the voice of the narrator blends harmoniously with those of a society which he otherwise despises. . . .

In *L'Amour impossible,* several themes of Barbey's major novels are adumbrated, and the views on love and passion expressed during later years will differ little from what has just been presented; these views will be developed with greater forcefulness and their artistic expression will go far beyond what is found in this early period. *L'Amour impossible,* like any other work by Barbey, contains variations on the themes of love, passion and sensuality; but the nexus of passion, cruelty, evil, and religion — the most essential element in the works as a whole — is here severely constricted by the setting and by the choice of characters. A psychological duel between a coquette and a dandy was hardly the ideal subject for Barbey. The subject, of course, does make it possible to evoke the transformative power of passion; but whereas in *L'Ensorcelée* or in the *Diaboliques* the result is tragedy, we are left here with mere pathos. Yet *L'Amour impossible* has more than an archaeological value, its author having succeeded in showing the dehumanization wrought by pride and cynicism and the ludicrous solitude of two individuals linked by a hybrid feeling which is mutual need without being passion. Because he has shown these, because he excels here as a portrait-painter, and because he has raised the question of how to recognize and define love, he has earned our praise, even though we may not share the world-view evinced by the novel: woman is a reptile, love is a duel, and the vampire of ennui is life's governing force.

IV   *Du Dandysme et de G. Brummell*

Barbey's personal dandyism, his moderately successful attempts to be the psychologist of "le noble Faubourg" in *La Bague d'Annibal* and *L'Amour impossible,* his obsession with Brummell were contributing factors which led to the idea of a treatise. Furthermore, in 1843, he was writing articles on ladies' fashions for *Le Moniteur de la Mode,* discoursing for example, on the relationship between elegance, grace, and beauty. Criticized by the editors as too metaphysical for the readership, Barbey stopped writing for *Le Moniteur;* but his interest in the psychological implications of elegance and dandyism did not wane. The initial idea had been a biographical sketch of Brummell, but Barbey quickly recognized the potential for a work of broader scope, namely a treatise on the theoretical aspects of dandyism; and so he moved beyond biography to an essay on dandyism and the formulation of a theory of Brummell's life. We shall see that the biography remains well-documented, nonetheless; for Barbey proceeds from anecdotes and intimate details, demonstrating a knowledge of the innermost recesses of Brummell's personality and using anything which might shed light on the true meaning of the man's life.

"The influence of Brummell could well be the subject of a book which Stendhal forgot to write and which would have tempted Montesquieu," Barbey states in the dedication of his work (II, 1429). The mention of these two prestigious names suggests the importance of the subject for the author who would study dandyism as a sociological phenomenon of which Brummell is the most perfect instance. The work contains an abundance of ideas and a brief summary hardly begins to suggest its richness. Since dandyism is viewed as an outgrowth of vanity, the book opens with a brief *apologia* for vanity. Since human feelings derive their value from their social importance, nothing, according to Barbey, could be of greater social worth than that harrowed search for approval which, in more important matters, is called love of glory, and in lesser ones vanity. Love, friendship, and pride are all centered upon an individual while vanity takes everything and everyone into account; yet, because of its fear of true feelings, society refuses to give vanity the place it deserves. When vanity in turn shows its own self-satisfaction, it becomes conceit; dandyism, a kind of conceit, is an English expression of vanity; the strength of British originality, impressed upon human vanity, has produced dandyism. In the first edition, Barbey insists that because of profound differences between the British temperament and the French, it is impossible for the latter to do anything more than to ape the former; and he distills the essence of British dandyism without confusing it with its French variation.

It is not merely the art of fashion, a bold and felicitous dictatorship in matters of dress and external elegance, it is a manner of being, made up entirely of nuances, "as always happens in very old and civilized societies, when comedy becomes so rare and when propriety barely triumphs over ennui" (II, 674). Dandyism results precisely from the struggle between propriety and ennui, and one of its most general characteristics is to produce the unexpected. Yet it must not be mistaken for eccentricity, Barbey declares rather surprisingly (II, 675); for it consists in playing with the rules of propriety, while respecting them, suffering from them, alternately dominating them and being dominated by them, which of course requires all the suppleness of grace. Such was Brummell's gift, and he was living proof of the truth that ". . . if the wings of Fancy are clipped, they will grow again, one and one half times as long" (II, 676); for we must bear in mind that much of Brummell's success is attributable to the all-pervasive ennui of the British aristocracy.

In his brief socio-historical overview of the society which helped to bring about dandyism, Barbey insists on the importance of grace which came into England from France with the Restoration of Charles II, and which clashed with the uncompromising seriousness and rigidity of the Puritans. Grace was accompanied by a growing taste for mockery and corruption, and those in whom these elements were combined were called "Beaus" — the very name bearing witness to the French origin of the phenomenon. Among them, Bolingbroke stands out as the only real dandy before Brummell — Bolingbroke who had the boldness of behavior, the sumptuous impertinence, the preoccupation with effect, the constant vanity, and who invented the motto of dandyism, "Nil mirari" ("To admire nothing"). Dandyism suited him perfectly, for it is an expression of freethinking in manners and propriety, just as philosophy is free thought in the realms of morals and religion (II, 681). Unmindful of an apparent contradiction, Barbey now asserts that the dandy establishes a new rule over the one which governs the most aristocratic circles and compels the acceptance of this new rule which amounts to nothing more than the boldness of his own personality (II, 681–82). Is frivolousness involved? Yes, but that is merely "a hateful name given to an entire order of preoccupations which are essentially legitimate, since they correspond to real needs" (II, 682).

George Bryan Brummell (1778–1840) was the son of a wealthy British family visited by guests such as Fox and Sheridan; it is highly plausible that such men helped him develop his talents as a brilliant conversationalist. At Eton, his extreme concern for his attire and his cold langor earned him the nickname "Buck." Already he justified Machiavelli's maxim "The world belongs to the cold-minded" (II, 683). After Oxford, he entered the Tenth Hussars, commanded by the Prince of Wales, the future George IV whose favorite Beau Brummell quickly became. After serving in the royal wedding party, his success was assured, and he was lionized by the most prominent aristocrats.

Adulated, much sought after, he did not become a libertine, he did not succumb to whatever passions he may have had and thus maintained intact his freedom to cultivate his vanity. That he did not love is a fact which Barbey finds perfectly logical: "To love, even in the less lofty sense of the term, to desire, is to depend, it is to be a slave of one's desire. Even the arms which encircle you most tenderly are still a chain . . ." (II, 686). This is not to say that Brummell never conquered women, but "his triumphs had the insolence of disinterestedness" (*ibid.*) and Barbey sees piquancy in Brummell's punishing women for their "pretentions lacking in good faith" (*ibid.*) and in his stopping at the very limit of 'galanterie" (extreme courteousness with perhaps a touch of flirtation) a limit which women do not really expect men to respect. Such restraint produced surprise and enhanced Brummell's success even further, a success abetted too by his constant application of the famous principle, "In society, stay as long as you have not produced an effect; once the effect is produced, leave" (II, 687).

The details of Brummell's life matter far less for Barbey than an analysis of his power and of those aspects of the man which allowed him to be the supreme judge of fashion and manners. He had the genius of irony, which made him the greatest mystifier in England's history, and a gift for bringing out the grotesque aspects of virtually anyone, for causing the other person to expose his or her ridiculousness: "A somewhat ferocious pleasure; but Dandyism is the product of a society which is bored and boredom does not make people kind" (II, 694). His awesome influence Barbey ascribes to an uncanny talent for blending terror and fondness in equal doses, a terror inspired by impertinence, the range of which was too extensive to express itself solely in epigrams: his actions, attitude, gestures, even the sound of his voice expressed it too. The fondness is more complex and is due to the mood of the aristocracy in Brummell's England, which combined extreme refinement and secret corruption; and it was said of him that he was too generally offensive not to be sought after. Barbey sees in this attitude the need to be beaten which sometimes takes hold of powerful and debauched women (II, 715). Indeed, a success which persisted for twenty-two years could not have been achieved, had it not corresponded to a real human need concealed beneath social conventions.

Of Brummell's falling-out with the Prince, of his mad passion for gambling which brought about his decline and ultimate financial ruin, Barbey sets forth merely the essentials. The same is true of Brummell's self-exile to France to flee his creditors and of his pathetic death in an asylum. To the very end of the "treatise," reflections of the "moraliste" demonstrate the author's intention to analyze, to comment or judge. Thus, during Brummell's exile, some wealthy English friends provided him with financial assistance out of a sense of gratitude for the pleasures *he* once provided — a logical action, for "... isn't giving them a bit of pleasure the greatest service one can render to societies which are bored?" (II, 707).

With palpable regret, Barbey notes the revival of Puritanism in modern-day England, the haughty phariseeism, the triumph of cant resulting in the death of Fancy, and the apparent demise of dandyism. No, he sighs, there will never be another dandy like Brummell, but there will always be men like him, for they are as eternal as capriciousness, giving intelligent people the pleasure to which they have a right, "Androgynes of History, no longer of Fable, among whom Alcibiades was the most beautiful type in the most beautiful of nations" (II, 717).

The "treatise" represents a crystallization of Barbey's views on the subject early in his career. Since dandyism was to be a lifelong preoccupation, and since the man himself was a living paradox, one can well understand the evolution and the sometimes contradictory nature of his views. Thus, while criticizing the frivolousness of the external phenomenon, he often defends it as the cult of form. There is no contradiction, however with regard to the *internal* phenomenon; for as its theoretician, historian and practitioner, he will constantly strive to improve upon it, perceiving it as a psychological discipline, a code of ethics, the mark of the superior man, an aristocracy of the soul, without relation to any particular society.

In time, he will come to see greater possibilities in dandyism, making pleas for a new dandyism, more moral, more intense, broader and more human. By the eighteen-fifties, he is criticizing the British for having made it so narrow and inhuman; in the Preface to the 1861 edition of the "treatise," he will argue that Pascal was a dandy, as was Rancé, the seventeenth-century Trappist; to the 1879 edition, he adds a short text entitled "Un Dandy d'avant les dandys," in which the principles of dandyism are applied to the seduction of a Princess, Mademoiselle de Montpensier, "la Grande Mademoiselle." In general terms, dandyism came to mean a philosophy of elegance, in which Barbey saw a rebuttal to bourgeois mediocrity and vulgar pragmatism. Elizabeth

Creed expressed it well when she wrote about "the revolt of the imagination against the seriousness *(gravité)* of the conformists: the dandy's cane rises against the bourgeois' umbrella."[2]

V *Conclusion*

Barbey's dandyism has suffered from the same misapprehension as dandyism in general. For most of his contemporaries, it consisted in nothing more than externals — outlandish attire and unyielding haughtiness — but the privileged few have access to the mystery of his soul knew otherwise. That he craved the distinction which noble birth and wealth would have brought him is undeniable; being blessed with neither, intensely scornful of his era, he found partial compensation in dandyism. But as the Treatise indicates, there is a certain asceticism in all of this, an ethic not unrelated to stoicism or to a philosophy of detachment, echoing Emerson's idea of self-reliance, with an emphasis on independence and fierce individualism. Dandyism itself is only one aspect of his aloofness, of his refuge from an ugly world — and in this respect it is closely allied to his Catholicism. Had he not written to his friend Trébutien in 1851: "Scorn for my fellow-men pushes me with infinite force into the bosom of our mother the Church, outside of which there is no salvation, either for Eternity or in Time"?[3]

CHAPTER 3

Normandy and Catholicism:
From Une vieille maîtresse *(1851)*
to Un prêtre marié *(1865)*

BARBEY d'Aurevilly had come to Paris as an enormously ambitious young man stultified by his native Normandy and his Catholic faith; during the eighteen-forties, he revolted against the constraints of "official" dandyism and the superficiality of Parisian life. He was increasingly repelled by the mediocrity of his era, its hypocrisy, its philistinism and the spread of bourgeois values. This revulsion was abetted by his readings: Joseph de Maistre and Balzac made him view the Roman Church as a principle of order and authority, while Walter Scott legitimated regionalism in literature. The confluence of these forces gave him a new outlook on Normandy which he came to recognize as a symbol of tradition in an age of chaos, of authenticity in a time of artificiality; his true identity began to emerge, for his ties to Paris were very recent, whereas Normandy, the land of his forebears for countless generations, formed an integral part of his innermost self. There was nothing affected or constricting in this spiritual return to his native province: it freed him from the tyranny of an oppressive present and this emancipation was facilitated by his memories of legends and tales heard in childhood. These would be completed by reading regional histories and personal accounts of the Crown's last defenders in the west of France. He conceived a cycle of historical novels dealing, precisely, with the staunch resistance of the Chouans, but history became largely a springboard for his unruly imagination; the Chouans, the members of the provincial nobility, various royalist sympathizers, the women associated with them — all acquired grandeur and mystery as they receded in time. They

58

came to seem larger than life and as such they could serve to embody yet another of Barbey's obsessions: passion — more specifically excessive passion which includes the exceptional, the bizarre, the paroxysmic. While the cycle of historical novels never materialized, Barbey's musings on regional history were transformed into enticing narratives about tragic passions, most often with members of the old nobility as protagonists and with Normandy as a setting.[1]

I Une vieille maîtresse

The passage from Paris to Normandy is effectuated in *Une vieille maîtresse,* a pivotal work in which the author's curiosity about psychological anomalies is combined with his fascination with the mysterious, both being used in an analysis of an appropriate subject, sado-masochistic love. The literary antecedents of the work are easier to establish than its origins in Barbey's personal life, since the lack of reliable documents has limited his biographers to brief remarks about an affair with a Spanish woman in the mid eighteen-forties. It has been ascertained however that Barbey was quite taken by Benjamin Constant's *Adolphe,* of which *Une vieille maîtresse* can be read as an antithesis, to the extent that the former is clinical, coldly analytical and devoid of feeling in mode or method. He was also impressed by George Sand's *Leone Leoni* which deals with a woman's love for a man despite his moral degradation; in addition, he had gained from Balzac a new awareness of fiction's potential for complexity and of the expressive value of externals, while Byron's influence is manifest in flashes of satanic passion.

Recognition of the work's literary merits is far more extensive today than during the novelist's lifetime: well received by Théophile Gautier and Baudelaire, but damned by Champfleury, the theoretician of Realism, for its alleged stylistic debauchery and blatant immorality, the novel raised anew the issue of art and morality. The atmosphere surrounding the debate was clouded by the untimely publication, a few weeks following the novel's appearance, of Barbey's *Les Prophètes du passé,* a thunderous apologia of Catholic royalist writers. His defense, published in the form of a Preface to the 1865 edition of the novel, is a statement about Catholicism and the rights of the Catholic novelist. Much as Stend-

hal proclaimed that a novel was a mirror drawn along a highway
and that the mud reflected in the mirror should be imputed to the
inspector of roads rather than to the person holding the mirror,
Barbey argued that literature reflects the human heart in which, of
necessity, one finds passion; art and passion are therefore inseparable, and Barbey insisted that he had condemned the very passion
he had described. Furthermore, if Catholic artists were to accept
the advice of the freethinkers and omit passion from their works,
then they could be justly accused of not being in touch with reality.
Catholicism, according to Barbey, is all-encompassing, the very
opposite of prudishness or puritanism, and certain works like
Michelangelo's "Last Judgment" contain elements offensive to
Protestant sensibilities. The Church affords all the latitude needed
by Art, so long as the artist does not preach vice or error; Barbey
makes other assertions perhaps more debatable to theologians than
the foregoing, e.g., the morality of an artist lies in the strength and
truth of his description and truth can never be a sin. This criterion
of truth applies even to the seductiveness of vice and the eloquence
of passion, for Catholicism, as the science of good and evil, scruti-
nizes the human heart and this, according to Barbey, is what the
author of *Une vieille maîtresse* has done.

Whether from the standpoint of French literary history or from
that of Barbey's work, the importance of this controversial Preface
is quite apparent: more than a century after *Une vieille maîtresse,*
the issue of morality in literature remains as unresolved as the
debate on the exact nature of Barbey's religion. In his Preface, he is
pleading *pro domo* only in part, and the soundness of certain arguments could hardly be contested by objective analysts; who would
quarrel with his assertion that the Church can ill afford to prohibit
the description of passion? Yes, the dichotomy between his novels
and his criticism is glaring, for there is no denying that he found
delight in describing passion in considerable detail, forbidden
passion made alluring by the savor of sin. To evoke the savor of sin
is to conjure up memories of Baudelaire, not solely of the poet who
sought to extract beauty from evil, but of the insightful observer
who expressed rather succinctly the dual aspect of human nature:
"There is in every man, at every hour, two simultaneous postula-
tions, one toward God, the other toward Satan."[2] In his own attempts to extract beauty from evil, Barbey the indomitable pessi-
mist and extremist, chose to focus on the ultimate evil, that of

damnation, which is tantamount to saying that Barbey's obsession with passion is comprehensible only within the framework of the Church's teachings on Heaven and Hell.

Une vieille maîtresse opens on a note of uncertainty and closes on one of ambivalence. The Marquise de Flers is about to marry off her grand-daughter, Hermangarde de Polastron, to Ryno de Marigny, a fashionable young womanizer, despite the objections of her friend the Comtesse d'Artelles. Ryno ends his ten-year liaison with Vellini his old mistress; the nature and depth of this relationship are revealed to Mme de Flers by Ryno himself in a lengthy and detailed confession. After hearing him out, the Marquise shares his conviction that the affair is over, and allows the marriage to take place. Ryno and Hermangarde spend the first months of their married life in perfect bliss at the estate of the Marquise in Normandy, until Vellini appears and the mysterious bonds uniting her and Ryno are found to have endured. Vellini settles into a fisherman's hut to facilitate frequent contacts with Ryno; Hermangarde learns the truth, survives a stillbirth and, abandoning hope, loses her trust in Ryno, despite his insistence that he still loves her. The conclusion offers two interpretations, the Norman fisher-folk believing in the magical powers of Vellini, while members of the Parisian *haut monde* prefer a less fanciful explanation.

Vellini, in the words of the novelist, is "child, woman, animal, Chimera, a blend of so many things so divinely molded."[3] References to her uniqueness occur repeatedly; Barbey knows, for instance, that we can accept at face value the judgment of Prosny, an old rogue who has had a half-century of experience with women: ". . . Vellini has no analogue in my repertoire of memories. Nothing can be understood about her! She's a logogriph, a hierogliph, a Chinese puzzle, and perhaps it is all of that which accounts for her power!" (p. 232). Sphinx, Chimera, *femme fatale,* she nevertheless lacks that stunning, seductive beauty one commonly associates with her type; indeed, we are consistently assured that she has no beauty whatsoever. That life which is in her, that vivaciousness, her expressiveness more than compensate for her physical ugliness. She has intensified the life-force in herself by going counter to accepted manners in developing her instincts to the fullest, so that there is something excessive and wild about her. Giving birth to the child sired by Ryno, she does so "like a creature of the desert, like a daughter of nature " (p. 309). This same unconventional attitude is evident when she decides to burn the body of the deceased child. Small wonder that this wild creature with bronze-like skin and the eyes of a wounded eagle should make love with the savageness of a tigress (p. 301).

This profound kinship with nature is however merely one aspect of Vellini, for these instincts were developed freely and knowingly. She moves about with ease and cunning in the society she has rejected and she knows that to keep a man, youth, beauty and kindness are far less useful than the art of keeping him interested, amused and — most important — worried. Given the intensity of her inner life, it is no surprise that she should attach so much importance to sight, the least material of all the senses; when Ryno leaves her to be with his wife, she recalls to him the words of the Bohemian song: "To see is to have," to which she adds the prophetic words: "When I see you, I will have you" (p. 460). She also shares the macabre power given to the Zahuri of the Spanish legends, which consists in seeing the decomposition of the body of the beloved beneath the earth and the flowers which will some day cover it (p. 312). For Barbey, the thought of passion invariably brings thoughts of death.

The richness of this inner life has other facets besides the sinister or the ghoulish. Acutely aware of a man's needs, she becomes the mistress of mistresses, perpetually renewing herself, drawing from a store of inexhaustible resources, dispensing unknown savors, unprecedented aromas, so that, alone, she is worth an entire harem. In the nineteenth century, the age of ennui, such an homage is staggering. Creature of the dream, Vellini's power exercises itself on the novelist himself, who writes that she "became beautiful again" when, angry with Ryno, she threw into her fireplace the medallion containing his portrait (p. 249) — this, after we have been reminded so relentlessly of her lack of beauty. Pity, too, is a weapon she wields astutely, as when she sheds a tear over Hermangarde's misfortune, thereby sympathizing with Ryno who is torn but will be touched by an expression of compassion on the part of his mistress who thereby reaffirms her moral ascendancy over him (p. 491).

To define the specific nature of this relationship, the novelist sometimes seems to be at a loss in the face of the enigma he has created, but his own astonishment too becomes creative. When he invokes a secret magnetism or a blood-pact to explain the persistence of passion, he is adding elements to one level at which the story can be read — the level of the magical, the bizarre, the exotic, with Vellini, a mystery-woman from far-off Malaga in Spain for a heroine. On a psychological level, the story is of course more plausible if Barbey is seen as a forerunner of the many writers of the eighteen-eighties and nineties whose protagonists were more blasé, more intense in their quest for new and unusual sensations than those of earlier generations. Vellini's voice, for example, awakens "the instinct of guilt-laden pleasures — the dormant dream of fabulous pleasures" (p. 274). The statement evokes unsuspected depths of repression, of Christianity, if we agree that guilt is an important part of the Judaeo-Christian heritage. Is it not the doing of Christianity that has put to sleep the dream — yes, even the very dream — of pleasures so inexpressible that we associate them with fable? There are other such evocations, in Barbey, of the pagan substratum in Christianized man.

While many of Barbey's libertines, insatiable in the frenzy of their emancipation, are left, blasé, with a perpetual need to seek ever more refined delights and pleasures, Ryno has been blessed with pleasures not only unprecedented and unexpected, but seemingly unattainable. Yet, the metaphysical, the cerebral, are not the dominant notes of this relationship: the passion is savagely physical, but without the habitual consequence of satiety; physical possession, usually so murderous for passion, gives Vellini an overpowering hold on Ryno after his marriage and will eventually bring him back to her. Even after an affair lasting more than ten years, after his marriage to a raving beauty whom he adores, the memory of the sensations Vellini can give will go on haunting, torturing him — the memory and the promise of inexhaustibly novel pleasures.

Barbey doubtless found great delight in the paradox of attributing almost superhuman power to a woman who was unspeakably ugly; his insistence upon this ugliness can hardly be overemphasized. Ryno himself sees two women in Vellini: "a being whose movement and life are dazzling" and "a being without radiance, the thin little yellow woman" (p. 278); without blushing, he admits his preference for the latter. With sheer delight, Barbey takes up the theme over and over, betraying his fascination with passions of an exceptional nature, evoking the unbelievable marvel of Vellini's ugliness (p. 268). Fully conscious of his depravity, Ryno confesses: "There are passions [amours] which corrupt everything in one's

soul .... I reached the point of loving, in the beloved, only that
which was the least beautiful'' (p. 278). Had she been diseased, he
would have loved her more, he would have loved precisely that part
of her which would have been diseased, would willingly have given
up polished marble for rotting clay. One does not explain away the
paradox, the mystery of Vellini; it is the part of wisdom to quote
Ryno's rhetorical questions:

Was she, for me, in a different order of sensations, one of those burning
seasonings after which everything seems insipid and tasteless? Like those
Javanese women who chew betel and give a pungent pleasure to European
men who never forget it once they've tasted it, could it be that Vellini, that
sangre azul of an African Spain, with the sharp, incendiary caviar of her
caresses, had lit, in the very source of my life, that thirst for fire which
cannot be quenched with fire, even in Hell? (p. 517)

Enthralled by her ugliness, Ryno is no less fascinated by Vellini's
androgynous nature. Her mouth, shaded by a dark bluish down,
her extremely flat chest, her voice, so masculine as to be of doubtful sex, these are merely the more obvious of her androgynous attributes. On the occasion of the duel between Vellini's husband and
Ryno, it is the Señora herself who serves as her husband's second.
Is she repulsive to Ryno when she plays such roles? Much to the
contrary, for it is precisely then that her power attains its zenith;
whatever is unpleasant about her as a woman (her irregular shape,
her hardness, her excessive thinness), all of that disappears when
she is dressed as a man. Recovering from the wounds received during the duel, Ryno keeps envisioning her constantly in masculine
clothing. And he speaks even more plainly when he states: ''I was
the odalisk of our liaison and she was the sultan; that pleased her
... and pleased me also '' (p. 302). This reversal of sexual roles, if
not commonplace in Barbey, does not really surprise the seasoned
reader of these novels and stories; it has occurred already in *Ce qui
ne meurt pas* and will recur later, notably in the *Diaboliques*. In this
respect, it is difficult to disagree with Jacques Petit: ''... the unexpected image of the androgyne has not brought us very far from the
theme of incest. What Barbey, the man or the novelist, asks of love,
is protection, and protection presupposes or includes domination.
These women with a masculine bearing or rather who borrow a few
aspects of adolescent virility, must represent that need.''[4]

This blend of peculiar elements must appear strange enough already to readers unfamiliar with Barbey's work, but there are others, also essential, which, after prolonged reading, one comes to regard as obsessive, such as the diabolical. While the latter is not given the full development it will receive in subsequent stories, it does indeed deserve mention. Since part of Barbey's frame of reference is Roman Catholicism, which for many has traditionally equated making love with committing evil, and since Vellini incarnates extra-marital love, we can readily understand that she would be allied with the Prince of Darkness: "In her there was that redoubtable seductiveness which a devil can be presumed to have. Like the devil, she had a slender sexless bust, a sinister, ardent face, and that impressive, bold, somber ugliness — the only thing worthy of replacing lost beauty on the face of a fallen Archangel" (p. 278).

By definition, Satan is a fearsome creature because of his virtually unlimited potential for domination over any given human being. Sinister, cunning, immoral, Vellini emerges even more clearly as a Satan-figure if we recall the sexual ambiguity, the reversal of male-female roles and her domination of Ryno. The contentment he derives from being subjugated is especially evident when he gives her the key to his apartment, thus allowing her to imprison him at will. We find here, merely adumbrated, another idea cherished by the author, namely the perfect union of a man and a woman, a union so perfect as to end forever the war between the sexes. The idea is given fuller expression when this kind of oneness is momentarily achieved by Ryno and Hermangarde; it is a moment when "man gains so much in grace and the woman in power, a divine fusion of two souls..." (p. 390). Such is the logical, self-fulfilling consequence of the concept of the androgyne, but moments of perfection are exceedingly rare in these novels, the author being obsessed with the corrosive, destructive elements which subsist even in the most frenzied passion, the persistence of hate even in a love which has survived the adversities of time, distance and marriage.

The agressiveness is shared and the interpenetration of love and hate begins with the relationship itself. Seated next to her at an elegant supper, Ryno becomes impassioned and picks up her glass to drink from it, to feel the touch of her lips; violently wrenching the glass from him she cuts herself, admits the physical pain, Ryno agreeing that he too prefers it thus, the intensity of his hatred being equal to the intensity of his love; and, for the first time, he experiences a painful violent pleasure by responding with contempt to her own contempt (p. 274).

Ryno revels in being whip-lashed by her, musing that every blow received from a woman is an advantage to a man if he understands his position (p. 289). In the psychological world which their temperaments and personalities have created, this ruthless struggle is an ongoing necessity, Ryno needs to be dominated, content to assert himself occasionally, and Vellini needs to dominate, daunted in turn by his superhuman resilience, his indomitable assurance that he will conquer her. Initially her hatred is greater than her attraction to him, a frenzied hatred inspired by pride, a hatred which, after a short time, will need to be whipped up and exaggerated, as it begins giving way to something resembling love, love seen as a threat. When she recognizes that hatred will be powerless to overcome its opposite, Vellini capitulates. Yet pride and hate have permanently scarred the relationship, for Barbey observes that love forever bears the mark of its origins, people go on loving exactly as they began to love; hence in the case of Ryno and Vellini, love and hate will always co-exist. One would be reluctant to argue that of the two, love is the greater force, so intense is the hatred, particularly that of Vellini for Ryno; the man for whom she would have given her life must frequently disarm her of her dagger when she assaults him.

As may be inferred from the above, there is nothing simple about the mysterious bonds which unite Ryno and Vellini; two other elements play a preponderant role in Barbey's development of his subject: a blood-pact and the weight of the past. Ostensibly, Vellini alone believes in the effectiveness of the blood-pact, which consists of lovers drinking one another's blood as a means of sealing their union forever; she has inherited from her mother a religious belief in this old custom and Ryno accedes to this ritual of a pagan marriage, dismisses it scornfully as sheer superstition, but at times can find no other explanation for the durability of their relationship, particularly when the link between them subsists after the eclipse of love. For Vellini, the blood-pact is more than a talisman; it is akin to the bond of blood which exists between mother and child, it transcends the affective, placing their relationship beyond the realm of human contingency. Reminders of the blood-pact recur but none is quite as striking as the letter written by Vellini, in her own blood, on the page of an old missal, with the express purpose of wooing him away from his young wife: predictably enough, the stratagem succeeds — the "hieroglyphs of savage and voluptuous loyalty" (p. 461) must have been particularly effective — and the relationship is resumed, as if ordained by fate.

Much more would need to be said about the role of the past than space permits, for Ryno's ten-year liaison with Vellini is so violent, so total, so far beyond the laws of probability that its logical reverberations offer virtually unlimited dramatic potential which the novelist has exploited most dexterously. As with the blood-pact, the initiative of resurrecting the past belongs to Vellini and is motivated less by jealousy than by her fervent cult of the past. Having enticed Ryno to a rendez-vous, she confesses that she loves him no longer, but views his happiness with Hermangarde as an insult to their own past happiness and affirms that she, rather than Hermangarde, is his true wife, that the blood-ties will prevail, despite Ryno's love for his legal spouse. Dutifully enough, Ryno struggles to ward off this evil influence by proliferating expressions of love for Hermangarde, but discovers that the memory of the heart is more ruthlessly loyal than the memory of the mind; hence the past assumes a reality more vibrant, more alive, more alluring than the present. The resumption of their liaison legitimates his expectations, the present now measures up to the past, and Vellini's hold upon Ryno becomes definitive, despite his continued love for Hermangarde. One finds more than empathy in Barbey's attitude toward all of this (despite statements in his Preface about condemning forbidden passion), even if one considers only the explicit remarks made by the author in his own name, to the effect that the past never returns in vain (p. 423) and that "of all the realities of existence, the most powerful is the chimera of the past" (p. 480). These are hardly denunciatory statements and they are not unrepresentative of the author's attitude; if one adds other revealing remarks such as his allusion to the latent power of a woman one has ceased to love (p. 416) and his declaration that the flesh too has a memory of its own (p. 472), one begins to see the characters from within, one senses that in this fictional world the characters are perpetually living out the past.

Even the relationship between Ryno and Hermangarde amounts to a playing out of the consequences of the past. Before they meet, she is already under the spell of this man, who is the scandal of the

Faubourg Saint-Germain, seeing him first through the eyes of
Madame de Mendoze whom he is rejecting in favor of Vellini. The
effect of Ryno upon both the Comtesse de Mendoze and upon Hermangarde is comparable to that of the manchineel, a tree whose
very shadow was said to be lethal. Yet the woman herself is unjustly
victimized, for she has beauty, wealth, a prestigious name and the
moral strength which allows her to accept her fate with the stoic
silence of a Mater Dolorosa. The significance of her destiny clearly
exceeds the bounds of Barbey's quintessential pessimism; there are
intimations (p. 256, p. 498) that her short-lived happiness with
Ryno de Marigny transcends what is tolerable to Barbey's Jansenistic God and that it must therefore be atoned for; in a historical
perspective, her defeat is the defeat of a caste, for though she
embodies many of the virtues of the old aristocracy, she lacks the
perspicacity and the cunning which would have allowed her to
retain her power over Ryno. Despite her youth, she is a withering
branch on a dying tree.

Hermangarde has grown up as the protégée of the Marquise de
Flers, an aristocratic survivor of pre-revolutionary France, and
through the Marquise, Barbey expresses his regrets over the passing
of the Old Order. She provides precious insights into the vanishing
aristocracy's feelings, values and sense of *grandeur;* she is now in
her declining years, but we are afforded tantalizing glimpses of the
woman she once was — "a doctoress of love" (p. 397) for whom
love had been an art heightened by the poetry of the senses, an
obviously strong woman with a fondness for black satin sheets and
with an admirable sagacity in the politics of love. It is this conception of love as a form of personal statesmanship which she vainly
attempts to transmit to her granddaughter, seeing woman's problem less in terms of conquering a man than of keeping her conquest. Aware of the frailty of a woman's happiness, she professes
that women either abuse their power or quite simply do not know
how to use it.

But the Marquise is for Barbey much more than an egotistical
cynic; she embodies for him a heraldic past. The artfulness of her
speech, its exquisite refinement, offers the most tangible evidence
of her belonging to another age. A parallel is drawn between the
eighteenth and the nineteenth centuries, and once again the latter is
found to be wanting. Of course Barbey abhorred the ideas in vogue
during the age of the enlightenment, the ideas which brought down

the monarchy and the aristocracy. But at the very least, people in the eighteenth century could express themselves with caustic wit, spirit and sparkle; and in recording the words of the Marquise, Barbey is celebrating that very special mode of conversation which became extinct with the passing of the nobility. The ensuing vacuum was filled by the bourgeoisie, whose lesser crimes — still according to Barbey — included the enshrinement of inanity and of "gravité" (boorish seriousness).

In Parisian high society, however, the Marquise de Flers is an exception. As described in Barbey's previous novels, sincerity is met with cruel jeers in this milieu where "doctors of elegant corruption" (p. 380) make wagers on the durability of the marriage of Ryno and Hermangarde. Further, hypocrisy is rank, for even the Comtesse d'Artelles, the loyal friend of the Marquise and an otherwise solid person, finds Ryno's ultimate return to Vellini to be an abomination. Yet she is horrified only because Vellini does not belong to the "noble Faubourg Saint-Germain"; and her double standard becomes even more striking when she admits that, had the roles been reversed, had Madame de Marigny reconquered a lover lost through marriage, she would find that disloyalty acceptable (p. 549). Such are the values of those who have given up on life's potential for happiness, who have seen and done everything, who have become hopelessly, totally cynical and blasé.

Quite other is Normandy, with the refreshing, humanizing influence of its humble folk, so authentic, so straightforward and sincere in their use of patois, in their naive superstitions or in their legends. For we do not doubt their belief in "Le Criard," a nameless horseman who wanders along the coast on the eve of a storm or of a misfortune (pp. 414–15); nor can their sincerity be doubted when they narrate the tragic story of "la blanche Caroline" whose ghost returns periodically, seeking burial in Christian ground (pp. 441–46). Barbey excels too in describing the coastal village of Carteret (pp. 369–75), as well as the sea viewed from different angles and in varying moods; these obscure forces of external nature correspond to the perhaps darker forces within us which play such a major role in the shaping of our destinies. It is also significant that, just as the second part of the novel takes place in Normandy — which marks a major turning-point in Barbey's writing — so too, one level of the novel's meaning is that provided by these unpretentious "gens de la côte."

II   Une vieille maîtresse: *Conclusion*

Ultimately, the levels of the novel's meaning can readily be reduced to two; despite the emphasis placed upon the elements of mystery, such as the blood-pact or the intimating of predestination, the merits of the novel do not depend upon our willingness to accept the story of Ryno and Vellini as totally inexplicable. The modern reader is also likely to dismiss the passages about "les grandes passions" as Romantic rhetoric, but the fact that Vellini allows Ryno to be completely himself — while other women do not — is an extremely compelling argument in her favor and in that of Barbey. In addition, the novel makes a very strong case for the extraordinary influence with which the past can be endowed; in this instance, it is a living ghost, an irresistible, omnipotent force which goes against all logic and seemingly against the grain of life itself. As such, it is not totally unlike the force which moves the Great Gatsby.

III   L'Ensorcelée

The origins of *L'Ensorcelée,* published in 1855, are essentially the same as those of *Une vieille maîtresse.* Balzac and Scott provided literary models, while on a more personal level, Barbey's intense rejection of the present resulted in an idealization of the Norman past. Tales heard during childhood about the legendary Chouans served as an appropriate screen upon which to project his admiration for their inordinate strength and uncanny craftiness, for their individualism and savage loyalty to the Crown, but especially for the bizarre passions such men might inspire. Upon publication, *L'Ensorcelée* did not receive the acclaim it deserved. Aside from the grumbling about the work's dubious morality or its outrageous style, the novel met with almost complete indifference. There was one formidable exception: Baudelaire considered it a masterpiece.

One night, as Barbey was crossing the fearful moor of Lessay in the company of Maître Louis Tainnebouy, an accident compelled the two men to spend the night in the misty moor. At midnight, the tolling of church-bells signaled the mass of the Abbé de la Croix-Jugan, according to Tainnebouy, who believed in this local superstition; upon Barbey's request, his companion related the story of the ill-fated mass. The Abbé, a well-known Chouan, had once attempted to commit suicide, but succeeded only in inflicting upon himself serious wounds aggravated by a sadistic group of revolutionaries, so that he was hideously disfigured. Shortly afterward, stripped of his priestly privileges, he was compelled by his superiors to attend church ceremonies at Blanchelande to atone for having been an active Chouan and for having attempted suicide. The Abbé, still majestically imposing despite his disfigurement, made an extremely powerful impression upon Maîtresse le Hardouey, née Jeanne-Madelaine de Feuardent, a depossessed noblewoman who had married the well-to-do farmer Thomas Le Hardouey solely in order to avoid abject poverty. The noble blood in Jeanne responded to the innate nobility of the Abbé, notwithstanding the latter's total impassivity, and a tragic passion began. Jeanne, well aware of the sacrilegious nature of her attachment, would not desist, hoping only that she and the Abbé might be damned together. Her outraged husband, learning from a band of wandering shepherds endowed with the gift of prophesy that the Abbé was to be his nemesis, resolved to destroy him. Incapable of accepting rejection, Jeanne-Madelaine committed suicide and the Abbé, reinstated by the Church authorities, was shot dead while celebrating mass on Easter Sunday.

Normandy and Catholicism are the bedrock of *L'Ensorcelée;* every significant aspect of the work is related to one or the other, and it is sometimes difficult to dissociate them. The foregoing is attested to by the enormous importance of the *fantastique*, the use of local superstitions and of patois. It is also evident in the tragic relationship of Jeanne Le Hardouey and the Abbé de la Croix-Jugan which of course constitutes the basic plot. Even place-names (such as "Coutances," "la Haie-du-Puits," "Saint-Sauveur-le-Vicomte," "Sainte-Mère-Eglise) are pungently Norman, adding much to local color. The occasional mention of legendary figures like Rollon or Du Guesclin offers added proof of Barbey's fierce love for his region and of his determination to "faire oeuvre normande." The region is of such importance that Barbey devotes the first two chapters to a lengthy rambling evocation of the setting in order to set the tone, to create an eerie atmosphere. To this end, the moor of Lessay is admirably suited, with its solitary grandeur, its mournful desolation, its shreds of a primitive and savage poetry; it had also been the alleged scene of murders and of strange apparitions in a past not so remote as to preclude recurrence. Nearby there once stood the Abbey of Blanchelande, a bastion of monasticism from the twelfth to the eighteenth century when degeneracy replaced piety and irreverent chronicles were told about highly unmonastic activities taking place at the Abbey; thus the novel's parameters of mystery and transgression are apparent from the outset, and the preponderant role of the region in these first pages is to be maintained throughout.

IV   Atmosphere and Milieu

That the moor of Lessay should suggest the desolation, the agonizing solitude of an inner landscape is undeniable, but it also suggests even more obscure regions of the human soul, regions where dwells the *fantastique,* an idea of such import that it warrants careful elucidation. Early on, the author declares,

I have always had a great fondness for popular legends and superstitions, for in them lies hidden a deeper meaning than is commonly believed, a meaning unnoticed by superficial minds who seek only the imaginative appeal and a fleeting emotion in this type of tale. Of course the story told by the grazier [Maître Tainnebouy] contained elements of what is generally called "marvel" [le merveilleux] (as if the underside of everything human were not a marvel just as inexplicable as that which people deny, for lack of an explanation!). But his story also contained events produced by the clash of passions or the inveterateness of feelings, which give to any story the poignant, immortal interest of that phoenix of dotards whose repetitions are always new and which is called the heart of man. (p. 583)

The source of the *fantastique* matters little: even popular legends and superstitions are acceptable, so that Barbey with his pretentions to nobility, his aristocratic cant, his avowed dandyism, the man one would have thought least likely to do so, is now defending these popular phenomena and using them in his novels. It should also be pointed out that virtually everything in the above-cited passage points up what separates Barbey from most of his contemporaries; but in order not to alienate too many readers, he also underscores the purely psychological aspect of the novel he is about to relate, namely the "events produced by the clash of passions or the inveterateness of feelings." He is proceeding here with rare caution and restraint, acutely aware that he is leaving himself open to ridicule, strongly believing in these legends and superstitions, yet reticent about giving them such a crucial role in his story. Elsewhere (p. 584), he affirms his belief in a tradition of secrets handed down by initiates from generation to generation and in the intervention of occult evil forces in the struggles of humanity. All of this — legends, superstitions, secrets, occult forces — comes under the rubric of *fantastique* and Barbey accepted both the elitist and outmoded qualities of these beliefs; flaunting such unfashionable ideas was merely another manifestation of Barbey the quintessential rebel. Despite his felt need to proffer psychological interpretations of certain given phenomena, he remained only half-convinced of the ability of reason to account fully for the bizarre workings of extreme passion or other unusual occurrences.

There is indeed a marked hesitation in his use of the *fantastique,* and he pleads its case repeatedly, having recourse to psychology or physiology to give his narrative wider credibility. Yet it must be seen as a crucial, integral part of the novel, and to dismiss it out of hand would falsify the interpretation of *L'Ensorcelée.* Sometimes brazen in his use of the *fantastique,* he gives an important role in the novel to a tiny band of wandering shepherds endowed with occult powers and knowledge of secrets and sortileges. Capable of bringing misfortune to farmers who reject their services, they also possess the gift of prophesying doom; thus, while returning from Vespers where she has been stricken as though by lightning by the Abbé, Jeanne meets a shepherd who assures her that she will long remember the Vespers she has just attended. Later, as her husband is traveling through the moor, he witnesses a horrifying scene in a shepherd's magic mirror, a vision of his heart being grilled by Jeanne and the Abbé; the scene confirms his suspicions, he becomes mad with a jealous rage, and finally he kills the Abbé. The phenomenon of the shepherds, inadmissible on a purely rational level, must be seen as a means of suggesting the very real existence of supernatural forces, and their intervention in human affairs.

There is yet another phenomenon belonging to the order of the *fantastique* which is even more striking, and that is the mass of the Abbé, signaled by the Blanchelande church-bells whose tolling is apt to bring misfortune to anyone hearing it. The bells are first heard by the author and the narrator (Maître Louis Tainnebouy) as they are crossing the moor at night, and their ringing serves as the pretext for the narration of the story. At the very end of the novel, one year after the murder, the mass itself is witnessed by a certain Pierre Cloud returning home at night through the moor. Alone in the church, the Abbé tries in vain to finish celebrating his mass for he is incapable of consecrating the bread and wine, his face "more horrible than it had been while he was alive, so similar to those found in cemeteries when old graves are dug up and old bones are unearthed, except that the wounds which had marked the Abbé's face were engraved upon his bones" (p. 739). The lugubrious message is clear — the wounds suffered during a lifetime are endured by the damned throughout eternity, and the anguish felt by Pierre Cloud is transmitted to the reader by these added notations:

...the more he moved forward, the more disturbed he became... He would become confused and he would stop... Quite as if he had forgotten what he knew... Really! he didn't know any more! But he kept going, stumbling over every word and starting over again... Having reached the Preface, he stopped short... He took his head in his skeletal hands, like a man lost trying to remember something which can save him and who does not remember it! He swooned... He wanted to consecrate, but he let the chalice fall upon the altar, touching it as if it devoured his hands. He looked as if he were going crazy. Really! A dead man insane? Can the dead ever become insane? It was more than horrible! (pp. 739–40)

Besides a macabre realism, Barbey demonstrates here the most horrendous aspect of the Catholic *fantastique,* the predictably futile efforts on the part of a man who has been damned, to transcend his torture; let us note too the sadistic irony of that torture — the savage cruelty of depriving a priest of his ability to celebrate mass. Through his repeated and sometimes spectacular use of the *fantastique,* Barbey expresses his firm belief in the supernatural; through his embodiment of this belief in human forms, he lends it a measure of plausibility, and makes it unerringly clear that his work will be grossly misunderstood if the *fantastique* and the supernatural are not taken into account.

Another dimension of *L'Ensorcelée* which makes the novel seem even more remote from the modern-day reader is the cult, the *sacralisation* of the past, through which Barbey manifests his rejection of the present. The events of the story take place shortly after the Revolution — hence a full half-century before the novel was written — and these events, as we have seen, are shrouded in the *fantastique,* which itself dates back to time immemorial. For

Barbey, the past has about it a mysteriousness and therefore a grandeur and a poetry which the banal present can never have, especially when the present and the past are juxtaposed. With the passing of the years, this cult of the past becomes more intense as his conviction grows that human history moves inexorably in a downward spiral away from all greatness and that human weakness simply hastens the fall. In the case of certain families, such as that of Jeanne, degeneracy had set in several generations earlier, hence with her passing, the once noble and revered name of Feuardent would become extinct. Mostly lost forever, the past can only be recaptured by those who possess the intelligence and sensitivity to be aware of its value — those who belong to a spiritual elite, such as Jeanne and the Abbé who commune together in their aristocratic past.

The milieu of *L'Ensorcelée* is considerably less claustrophobic than that of previous novels, for Barbey wisely chose to include in this work representatives of the lower classes — peasants, servants, village gossips who, by speaking in patois, add a realistic touch, a note of authenticity. These peripheral figures also help make the central characters less ethereal; through them the story gains immediacy, it becomes more plausible, more firmly rooted in a universally recognizable human landscape. Their horror is understandably exaggerated, since they witness events without being aware of their causes, which are mysterious enough to minds less unsophisticated. But Barbey's attitude toward them is not the condescension we might have anticipated from a frustrated aristocrat, for by having these "little people" impute the death of Jeanne to the Abbé, Barbey recognizes the existence of a folk-wisdom capable of grasping more than a modicum of a complex truth. He goes yet further with his statement that "gossips, after all, are miniature poets who thrive on stories, unveiled secrets, mendacious exaggerations — the eternal sustenance of any poetry; they are the matrons of human invention who, in their own manner, shape the realities of History" (pp. 604-5). He also paints a moving portrait of Clotilde Mauduit ("la Clotte"), a paralytic old sibyl, ostracized for having once scorned the lower classes and who, though a commoner, had been the Herodias at the orgiastic revelries of the local nobility. Perpetually idolatrous of the aristocracy, she too lives in another age, playing hostess to the Abbé de la Croix-Jugan, whom she has known since youth. Ever worshipful of a noble name, she persists in calling Jeanne "Mademoiselle de Feuardent," ignoring the latter's marriage; for, to this extent at least, she can pretend that the past has remained intact. She is therefore the perfect confidante, but more importantly, she is for Jeanne a living link to a vanished past.

V   Characters and Plot

The Abbé Jéhoël de la Croix-Jugan is a mystery to the "little people" around him, the embodiment of solitude and the object of a fatal enchantment for Jeanne le Hardouey. Much like Barbey, he remains undaunted, unreconciled to the present, consistently attempting to bring back an irrecoverable past; he will not accept, he will not compromise, he will not surrender. He is a monolith, a marmoreal figure, yet credible, perhaps because Barbey expressed through him so much of his own inexhaustible scorn for the mediocrity of his era, his unbounded impatience over his personal powerlessness. Barbey too lusted for action but was condemned to inaction by the forces of history: the frustrated nobleman in him was also a frustrated Chouan, born too late to take part even in the final desperate rear-guard action.

Nor did Barbey have to "invent" the Abbé's pride or revolt, the pride which comes with noble birth, with a cultivated sense of caste, with the knowledge that history notwithstanding, one has been destined to command. The Abbé's revolt is directed primarily against the Revolution of course, which violated the foreordained order of things; but it is directed against the Church also for forbidding the spilling of blood, even the blood of its own enemies. His is an epic stature, and what is known about him is obtained largely by inference since the reader seldom has access to his private thoughts. As the youngest son of a noble family, he stoically observed the age-old tradition of becoming a monk, despite his lack of religious fervor; a thoroughgoing aristocrat, he was drawn to the orgiastic gatherings of noblemen such as Remy Sang d'Aiglon de Haut-Mesnil, but his own "debauchery" was limited to sullen drinking while those about him revelled; extraordinarily loyal to his vow of celibacy, he resisted the most overt and persevering advances of the noblewomen around him, the company of aristocrats offering adequate relief from his otherwise dull existence.

The warrior which he was meant to be responded to the call swiftly and passionately when the Revolution broke, and it is said that he killed as many revolutionaries as he had killed wolves in his days as a master-huntsman. Even after all reasonable hope for the royalist cause should be abandoned, he remains involved in guerrilla warfare as a Chouan; yielding finally to despair, he attempts suicide, fails, then submits externally to the penance imposed upon him by the Church. Despite the horrible disfigurement caused by his suicide attempt, he retains a commanding appearance, for his bearing is that of the old Normans, the one-time Kings of the Sea who in the ninth century had inspired the cry: "A furore Normanorum libera nos, Domine!" (p. 646). His life-style befits a religious and political outsider; hermit-like, he lives on the outskirts of the hamlet, is frequently seen at church by day, but by night he becomes the inscrutable horseman, going about mysterious errands — pursuing the impossible royalist dream. He is a man apart, redoubtable in his silver-spurred riding-boots, trusting only his pistols, his oldest companions — pistols with a cross on each barrel and a fleur-de-lys encrusted in each cross, signifying that the Chouan fought for God his Savior and for his lord the King of France.

Constantly Barbey plays up the hideous disfigurement and — particularly in the Abbé's relationship with Jeanne — the satanic overtones, obviously fascinated by the originality of his own inventiveness: "His hood dropped, and his Gorgonian head appeared, the broad temples trepanned by inexpressible sufferings, and the face upon which the radiating bullets had formed an intaglio of sun-like gashes. His eyes, ablaze and blinding, lit up his face, like a thunderbolt might light up a lightning-rod. The blood meandered, like a ribbon of flames, his eyelids burned, similar to the burning eyelids of a lion coming out of a conflagration. It was magnificent and atrocious both!" (p. 645). The length of this detailed description, its precision, its mannered yet dynamic style betray the extent to which Barbey was haunted by the massacred face of this man who had seemingly triumphed over death by courting it and who forever after was marked by wounds which were perpetual reminders of his defiance of death, wounds compared by Barbey to the most celebrated wounds ever recorded by History (p. 727).

Such a preposterously frightful appearance is logically associated by the peasants with the most frightful being of all, the Devil himself; and this association is closely related to one of Barbey's principal obsessions, satanism. Although the satanism of the Abbé exists solely in the minds of the peasants, since we are repeatedly told that his appearance reminds them more of the Devil than of God, there can be little doubt that Barbey intended him to be considered, at least in part, a Satan-figure. The idea of casting a priest in such a role must have seemed extremely ingenious to Barbey, but the idea is used here with great restraint and its full potential will not be exploited until the writing of *Un prêtre marié,* several years later. For the moment, Barbey transfers the burden of satanism to Jeanne by means of her forbidden passion for the Abbé.

The relationship between Jeanne and the Abbé is not analyzed in the novel itself, Barbey having assumed the role of which he is fondest, that of *conteur* ("story-teller"), feeling compelled only to set down the facts, leaving their elucidation and interpretation to the reader. Their first meeting takes place at Vespers, and she first lays eyes upon him while the antiphon "et statim veniet dominator" ("and soon the Dominator will come") is being sung, all of which points up Barbey's strong penchant for combining religion with passion. The Abbé's initial impression upon Jeanne is indeed one of domination; it is an extremely powerful impression to which her immediate reactions are a shudder, along with feelings of dizziness, terror, and anguished fascination. These quickly yield to a preoccupation described as diabolical (p. 608), a fatidical obsession, while the ugliness of this "baleful being" ("l'être funeste") is termed "grandiose" (p. 622).

The reasons for such bizarre behavior can only be inferred; and although they do not appear completely convincing at a psychological level, they do afford an insight into Barbey's conception of nobility. Until her meeting with the Abbé de la Croix-Jugan, Jeanne had been a most proper woman, the spouse of Maître Thomas le Hardouey, but submitted to her husband only in her external behavior. Occasioned by the Revolution, the marriage had been a tragic mismatch; Jeanne's sole alternative, pauperism, might well have been preferred if she could only have foreseen the depths of the guilt and revulsion which she was to experience, not only for marrying beneath her, but for marrying a man who had bought Church property, thereby aligning himself forever with the enemies of the Church and the aristocracy. Her grievous misalliance had been a psychological incarceration; and for having thus humiliated her family's name, she had been left disconsolate and at least sub-consciously ready for revolt.

During the brief initial meeting, the blood of Jeanne the noble-woman responded instinctively to the aristocratic presence of the Abbé de la Croix-Jugan. When she learned about his past, her feel-ing became one of enthusiastic admiration for the man who, despite his status as a priest, remembered only one thing when the Revolution erupted — his own nobility — and who defended the Crown at the risk of his soul. This then was the kind of man she should have married: one to whom she is fatefully and fatally at-tracted because of his total being — his ancestral past, his patrician blood, his prodigious strength of character, the tragedy of his ugli-ness itself. He also speaks the language of the nobility, still has the feelings of the nobility and is still secretly working for the royalist cause against all odds. One can then well imagine that she might develop for him "a grandiose, ideal and passionate interest" (p. 665), and that she would begin to assist him in his counter-revolu-tionary activities, acting as an intermediary between him and other isolated guerrilla leaders. By assisting him in this cause she does more than express her passionate love; she attempts to redeem her-self for her dishonorable marriage, and in so doing is true to her deepest self, for there is no other cause she believes in as deeply.

Yet she does not heed the warning of her confidante Clotilde Mauduit who beseeches her to avoid all contact with the Abbé lest she commit some irrevocable act, for paradoxically, her own moral strength lies at the source of her destruction; because she is strong and of superior breeding, she will not be horrified by the man's dis-figurement, will not allow it to stand in the way of an all-consuming attachment. With time, of course, she recognizes that her sense of caste and her quest for redemption have led her from what she regards as the heinous sinfulness of her marriage to a sacrilegious passion for a priest. With time also, the secret relation-ship loses its secrecy, the most horrendous tales regarding Jeanne and the Abbé are bruited about, as their clandestine meetings in the sacristy are made known and are given distorted interpretations by scandal-mongers and gossips, aware only of part of the truth, the villagers give ever more credence to rumors that Jeanne has been "bewitched."

In reality, the passion is not reciprocal. Jeanne's love remains unrequited. It is in fact doubtful that the Abbé is even conscious of

her love, for at least outwardly he appears to be all intellect and
will, a true monomaniac, fanatically obsessed with an ideal impossible of attainment. When finally he deems the ideal to be hopeless, he withdraws completely and stops seeing Jeanne, who is no
longer useful to him. The rejection proves to be fatal. Already his
unresponsiveness has caused Jeanne to live in a trance, unwilling to
heal, experiencing unspeakable suffering, shame and despondency.
His ultimate rejection of her produces a cataclysmic upheaval
resulting in a stupor resembling incipient paralysis followed by a
decision to end her life; but she has retained sufficient lucidity to
know that for loving a priest (a sin which, in her own estimation,
God Himself cannot forgive) she will be damned for all eternity.
Feeling that she has been psychically murdered by him, she goes
beyond her decision to die and makes explicit to her confidante her
will that he too be damned with her, since she anticipates that hell
with him would be preferable to life without him (p. 668); here we
may see an expression of supreme sadism.

VI *Evaluation*

In *L'Ensorcelée,* Barbey has created viable, memorable characters propelled to tragic ends either by fate or by their own wills.
Jeanne Le Hardouey is an absolute of passion; one senses in her no
tenderness, sentimentality or eroticism, simply a persistent frenzy
of passion whose feverish intensity never flags or wavers. The Abbé
Jéhoël de la Croix-Jugan belongs to a vanishing breed of royalist
desperadoes, totally committed to a cause as hopeless as the passion Jeanne feels for him. The work can easily be read on either of
two levels, neither one necessarily excluding the other. On the surface, it is the story of a bewitching, recognized as such by the humble folk, while on a different level, more credible to the modern
reader, we are here in the presence of an obsession closely resembling psychosis. With this venture into the realm of the pathologi-
cal, Barbey can be considered a precursor of Realism.[5]
Barbey is also to be commended for effectively exploiting local
superstitions, oral tradition and other manifestations of Norman
lore; in fact, *L'Ensorcelée* establishes Barbey as the first regional
writer of any consequence. In many respects, the work deserves to
be called a "mood novel" — perhaps the first in French literature
— for in the final analysis, it does become an *état d'âme,* a mood

which is a compound of eerieness, fear, anxiety and anguish. It remains, at least for this reader, an impressive novel with a strong incantatory power and also a novel which, by the reality it evokes, rehabilitates the spiritual aspect of literature, making of Barbey a forerunner of Huysmans, Bloy, Bernanos and Mauriac.

VII   Le Chevalier des Touches

Le Chevalier des Touches, published in 1864, relates an episode which took place during the last days of "la Chouannerie," that hopeless rear-guard guerrilla action conducted by the arch-royalist outlaws encountered in *L'Ensorcelée.* In the latter novel, the purely historical aspect was overshadowed by the strange passion of Jeanne Le Hardouey for the Abbé Jéhoël de la Croix-Jugan. Here, Barbey focuses primarily on specific historical incidents and without adhering strictly to historical truth, he succeeds in capturing the spirit and temper of "la Chouannerie," while skillfully weaving a love story into the fabric of the main story. This unlikely shift of emphasis from passion to heroism can be attributed to a sincere desire to exploit the abundant lore of the Norman past. Controlling his fascination with violent passion, however, was done to please the woman he hoped to marry (Madame de Bouglon); but it would prove to be temporary. The result was a work which can be loosely called a historical novel, free of eroticism, hence morally unobjectionable; as such, it came to be more widely read than his other works, earning the praise of Jules Vallès and Anatole France.

The novel begins with a lengthy description of the setting in which the story is told. During the last years of the Restoration (hence in the late eighteen-twenties), in Valognes, an aristocratic little town in Normandy, several friends have gathered in the salon of two elderly spinster-sisters, Mesdemoiselles de Touffedelys. The small group includes two noblemen, the Baron de Fierdrap and the Abbé de Percy, for whom the narrative is primarily intended, Aimée de Spens whose fiancé, Monsieur Jacques, was killed during the events about to be described, and the narrator, Mademoiselle de Percy, a participant in those events. In 1799, when "la Chouannerie" had been virtually defeated, the Republicans captured an important Chouan, the Chevalier des Touches. His comrades-in-arms resolve to liberate him, but their plan is foiled by an alert gaoler. Elaborate preparations are made for the second expedition which does succeed but at the cost of Monsieur Jacques' life. Des Touches seeks out the miller responsible for his arrest and metes out an unspeakably cruel revenge before embarking for England to resume his mission as a courier between royalist leaders in exile and those on the mainland. In the final chapter, Barbey relates his brief meeting with des Touches many years later, learning from him the reason why Aimée de Spens would always blush when hearing his name.

VIII   *Setting and Atmosphere*

Fully one-fourth of the novel is given over to describing, in considerable detail, each one of the persons who listens to it. Understanding this procedure is essential to understanding the novel, since we have here a fusion of technique and meaning. The events are not recounted merely to distract the Baron de Fierdrap and the Abbé de Percy who, like many noblemen, had emigrated to England during the Revolution. The events, though distant in time, are a high point in the lives of the others in attendance; hence the reader observes them in the process of reliving a crucial part of their common past. Time stops, is reversed, and the past is conjured up most vividly by a gifted narrator. Seated in a salon with furnishings so dated that they are no longer seen any more even in the provinces (at the time of writing, nearly a half-century later), the characters are in perfect harmony with this setting. Extremely serious about the events narrated, the persons involved and the values they represent, Barbey seems to be creating, in these early chapters, pastiches of his usual characters, the members of the old nobility whom he cherished dearly. Mesdemoiselles de Touffedelys offer the best example; sharing identical tastes in everything, each of these "two female Menechmi" (p. 750) is an exact duplicate of the other. One such aristocratic antique would hardly have made an impression, given Barbey's fondness for anachronisms, but the replication creates the effect of a caricature unique in all his work, particularly when we learn that Mlle Sainte de Touffedelys had spurned a request to marry because her sister had not found an acceptable suitor (*ibid.*).

Mademoiselle de Percy, when first presented, seems even more preposterous: "This woman was so remarkably grotesque that she would have been noticed even in England, the country of the grotesque, where spleen, eccentricity, wealth and gin are perpetually at work creating a carnival of faces compared to which the masks of the carnival of Venice would be crudely painted cardboard" (p. 751). This lightness of touch is seldom encountered in Barbey and the tone is altered when the author introduces the Abbé de Percy, and underscores the Abbé's social uselessness. Born to be a leader of men but stripped of any possible authority by the Revolution, he is still respected for his mental agility, his gifts of irony and wit. His life has acquired a gratuitousness like that of his friend the Baron de Fierdrap.

There is no lightness, no element of caricature in the person of Aimée de Spens whose deafness prevents her from hearing the narrative, yet whose presence heightens the reader's interest since the course of her life was tragically altered by the events retold. The last member of an illustrious family, she was once renowned for a beauty more stunning than Lady Hamilton's. Haunted, like Villon, by the phenomenon of vanished beauty, Barbey takes up the theme over and over: "With age, her dazzling beauty had become subdued and velvety like the rays of the moon" (p. 770). Younger than her companions, she might well be their contemporary if one considers her complete withdrawal from the world into a life made up of thoughts and memories kept sacred by remaining unshared. Resigned to being forgotten by the world, of which she has become oblivious (p.785), she has been faithful to her destiny of a "virgin-widow" (p. 769); and Barbey's wistful musings on her life's meaning tell us much about the man himself. Her strength and steadfast loyalty to an ideal — monarchy — and to her deceased fiancé make her a morally superior being whose life, ostensibly a failure, is in reality a defeat more triumphant than the victories of others (p. 772). When all of this is borne in mind, the purpose of her presence becomes clearer; for through her, the links between past and present are strengthened, the reader has a heightened sense that the past which has been lost is truly found again and is, for a few hours, relived.

So all-pervasive is the theme of time that it would be difficult to overstate its importance. In this as in other novels, the Revolution is seen as the Apocalypse, the definitive, irrevocable end of a millenium. The Abbé de Percy is the last offspring of his family, Aimée de Spens is the last of her breed, an era has ended, the final phase of the transition from the Old Order to the new has begun.

Implicit throughout the work (and often explicit) is a contrast between what was and what is, a melancholy contemplation of a
glorious past. Barbey exalts the Chouans for their sang-froid, their
intrepidity in attempting to bring back the monarchy. Praising the
Chouans made particularly good sense for Barbey who was both an
aristocrat and a rebel, since "la Chouannerie" was a revolt against
the newly established Republic in the name of the monarchy and
the aristocracy. Because "la Chouannerie" was a loosely-organized
form of guerrilla warfare, it encouraged the personal initiative of
exacerbated individualists at the same time as it demanded strong
dedication to a cause; the self had wide latitude, but was also involved in something far greater than itself.

We see here yet further evidence of Barbey's cult of strength,
authority, autocracy, and heroism, the very opposite of what he
saw in the rule of the bourgeoisie. The Restoration itself resolved
nothing, for the Bourbons failed to recognize the loyalty of the old
nobility. Thus the Baron de Fierdrap's reproach is quite under-
standable: "... we love them enough to be able to complain about
them. They are similar to the Stuarts and will end up like them.
They are just as flighty, just as ungrateful" (p. 761). Even in the
face of such gross indifference, the Baron and the people gathered
in the little salon retain the religion of royalty, they remain loyal
quand même. Such unswerving absolute loyalty is an attitude which
Barbey the extremist could only admire. He admired it all the more,
knowing that this loyalty increased the isolation of these people
who, having barely escaped the guillotine, were already isolated
from the rest of society because of their political beliefs.

At the very least, however, these people can commune together in
a common past, and this is why the narrative of Mlle de Percy is
frequently interrupted by the reactions of her listeners; this is why
too the novel at times becomes conversational. Communication at
the same profound level is still possible after several decades and
this increases the great delight she finds in her role, particularly
when, in response to the insistence of the Baron de Fierdrap, she reveals the names of the twelve members of the expedition. The
listeners' reaction indicates their state of mind: instinctively
"... the Abbé de Percy and M. de Fierdrap made the same movement, typical of noblemen. They could not remove their hats, since
they were bareheaded, but they bowed upon hearing the names of
the heroic troup, as if they were saluting their peers" (p. 799). Here

is a good example of the effects of the past upon the present, for the gesture indicates quite clearly that the values of these people have not changed and underlines the existence, however tenuous or pathetic, of a continuum from past to present.

IX *Characters and Plot*

Des Touches the man combines the best qualities of the Chouan with certain traits typical of many of Barbey's male characters. His indomitable will and fierce sense of duty remind us of Corneille's heroes; yet his true motives remain concealed, for whether he is a real zealot of the monarchy or a shiftless adventurer is never ascertained. Endowed with prodigious physical strength and "a heart made of oak" (p. 778), he has a beauty which is almost feminine, a fact hardly worth pointing out if it were mentioned only once. But Barbey stresses the point, accumulating details about the fairness of des Touches' complexion, his curly blond hair, his delicate angel-like face, his slender womanly figure. Even more curious, he was called "la belle Hélène" after being freed from jail (p. 759), an overt reference to Helen of Troy; in fact, Chapter II is entitled "Hélène et Pâris" and Barbey had considered giving his novel the title "L'Enlèvement" ("The Abduction"). In most novels, with varying degrees of explicitness, Barbey betrays his obsession with androgyny; and in the novel we are discussing, the feminine traits of des Touches are paralleled by the masculine characteristics of Mlle de Percy, one of his liberators.

Des Touches himself is seldom seen, and the reasons for his importance to the Chouans remain as obscure as the motives for his actions. His extraordinary importance to the Chouans is ascribed, somewhat vaguely, to his boundless resourcefulness, intrepidity and loyalty to the cause. Before his capture, he was constantly risking his life as a courier, crossing the Channel in the crudest of small boats during the worst of storms, seemingly capable of enchanting the waves to ensure his own safety. A master at guerrilla warfare, his lust for blood, his phenomenal speed and his deadly marksmanship earned him the nickname of "the Wasp" and made him one of the most sought after of all the insurgents. Paradoxically, the man presumed by the reader to be the hero or the protagonist makes only three brief appearances in the course of the novel, each one of them rather disquieting. He is first seen by Abbé de Percy on a rainy evening in Valognes just long enough to emerge from the darkness, to grasp the Abbé's arm and shout hoarsely: "I am the Chevalier des Touches; they're an ungrateful lot, aren't they?" (p. 760). The face is described by the Abbé as "uglier than mine! a devastated, bearded, whitened face with wild flashing eyes..." (*ibid.*). He vanishes into the night, the Abbé goes on to visit the Touffedelys, and this ghostly apparition will serve as the pretext for the lengthy narrative of the Chevalier's liberation thirty years earlier.

Having been freed from prison, des Touches decides to seek revenge against the miller who betrayed him and to avenge the death of Monsieur Jacques. Returning to the scene of his capture, he lays hold of the miller, ties him to one of the arms of the windmill and stands back to admire his handiwork in the presence of his liberators. This imaginative cruelty will be refined by the time Barbey writes his *Diaboliques,* but it shows the author's fascination with cruelty, violence and sadism; the incident makes us regret that we are not given insights into this type of mind, especially since in his last appearance, des Touches is in an insane asylum where he has been confined for two decades. Since he first heard the story of the liberation as a child, Barbey had obtained additional bits of information about des Touches, all the while becoming increasingly curious about him, finally deciding to seek him out:

The state in which I would find this heroic man, completely dead and rotting away in the most ghastly of sepulchers — a crazy house! — was an added reason for giving myself this spectacle. It is so good to soak one's heart in a scorn for things human, especially glory, which bluffs those who rely on it and believe that it is not deceitful.

So there came a day when I was able to see this Chevalier des Touches and, in my own mind, to relate his young, willowy, terrible figure, like that of Perseus cutting off the Gorgon's head, to the figure of an old man besotted by age, insanity and all the oppressions of destiny. (p. 867)

Several of Barbey's obsessions are brought together in this passage: the destructive effects of time and betrayal, the ephemeral nature of glory, psychic disintegration, and psychological anomalies. With regard to the latter, the modern reader may well be surprised by Barbey's truly remarkable precision, which has allowed commentators to describe des Touches as a leptosome in a chronically delirious state with a markedly schizoid behavior.[6] These obsessions point to Barbey's lifelong preoccupation with tragic failure, a failure which, in the case of des Touches, has been made all the more tragic, given the betrayal of ambitions legitimated by countless heroic deeds performed in the service of the monarchy. The destiny of Aimée de Spens is somewhat less tragic. Except for Calixte Sombreval in *Un prêtre marié* (*A Married Priest*), she is the only "celestial" woman in all of Barbey's work, "celestial" being used by Barbey as an antonym of "diabolical" — a type he clearly preferred. Aimée de Spens is the archetypal isolated figure. Sharing the same unfashionable political beliefs as the other characters in the novel, she has been prevented by historical circumstances from fulfilling her anticipated role as the wife of her fiancé, Monsieur Jacques, killed during the liberation of des Touches, hence the appropriateness of the term "virgin-widow" to describe her. It would be facile to say that a person of such extraordinary beauty could easily have married someone else. Women of her caliber, cast in a mold of total dedication, give themselves only once, to one man only; and if the death of that man should precede the consummation of the marriage, they do not seek elsewhere, they remain faithful to that man until their dying day. According to the author, Aimée de Spens was created for "God's pleasure alone" (p. 784) and that is our sole indication that her existence was not completely lacking in purpose. In addition, she is afflicted with a deafness which at times is complete; and in being cut off from even the most elementary form of communication, her isolation is total.

The ludicrous appearance of Mlle de Percy in the first part of the novel is vindicated by her heroic past so that once again, through her, the present is unfavorably compared to the past. She is, for Barbey, much more than a spoof of the strong woman with masculine characteristics, for she is the only female narrator in his entire work. The uniqueness of this important role can be interpreted as a highly unusual homage. After the failure of the first expedition to save des Touches, this "Amazon of la Chouannerie" proves to be an excellent choice to replace the missing Chouan. As a woman, she is a misfit, admitting that she should have been a man ("je ne suis guère qu'un homme manqué," p. 802); she preferred fabricating bullets rather than dresses, and even in her later years she still curses like a dragoon — a habit she justifies quite easily: "Didn't I fight long enough in honor of God and His Holy Church for Him

to overlook bad habits acquired during His service..." (*ibid.*).
This is not untypical of the French aristocrats' attitude toward
God, as further illustrated by Louis XIV's statement after losing
the battle of Malplaquet: "I had rendered enough services to God
to have the right to hope that he would treat me better than he
has!" (*ibid.*).

After this lengthy introduction, the depiction of the action itself
is traditional, linear. The main plot consists of the two attempts to
liberate des Touches, the secondary plot dealing with the ill-fated
love of Aimée de Spens and Monsieur Jacques. The novel is high-
lighted by several scenes and incidents worthy of becoming anthol-
ogy pieces and of being analyzed in detail, but which can only be
mentioned briefly here. In Chapter V, the story of the first attempt
to free des Touches is a highly successful blend of realistic description and epic narrative. The fair at Avranches is portrayed so
vividly that one can easily visualize the scene and hear the wheat-
merchants and the animals; indeed, if one were to assemble a
collection of "Scènes de la vie normande," these pages would be
essential. The brawl provoked by the Chouans at Avranches, as
part of their strategy, is reminiscent of Rabelaisian mock-epic combat scenes and also anticipates Zola's crowd scenes. The chapter
dealing with the second expedition is particularly memorable for its
description of Coutances, the town where des Touches has been
transferred and is to be guillotined. Here again Barbey demonstrates his ability to capture a mood, this time the mood of a small
Norman town slumbering in the quietude of a misty moonlit night,
in a profound silence broken only by the soft-voiced warnings of an
old woman emptying a chamber-pot from her upstairs apartment in
a motion so slow "that the drops of the liquid she was pouring
could have crystallized before hitting the ground, had it been a bit
colder" (p. 837). Her repeated warnings of "Watch out for the
water!" and the extreme caution of her slow motions provoke quiet
laughter in the reader and in the Chouans, and make us wish that
Barbey had cultivated his comic gift.

Between the two expeditions, one finds the most moving scene of
the novel, a scene which brings together both the main and the
secondary plots. Desiring to become something more than the
fiancée of M. Jacques, Aimée de Spens, at the Touffedelys manor-
house, on the eve of the departure, dressed in a white wedding-
gown, declares to those in attendance:

'Be my witnesses, Gentlemen' — ever more touching and majestic with every word, — 'that I, Aimée-Isabelle de Spens, Countess of Spens and Marquise of Lathallan, here present, I, this day, take for spouse and master Monsieur Jacques, presently a soldier in His Majesty's service. Compelled by the necessity of these sad times which have neither churches nor priests to ratify and consecrate the solemn engagement which I am making today, I have decided, with complete freedom of soul, to vow obedience and fidelity to Monsieur Jacques and to plight my troth to him, at least in the presence of yourselves, who are Christians and Gentlemen — for in times of strife, Christians are almost priests!' (pp. 829–30)

When she laments the lack of a cross upon which to swear her allegiance, two of the noblemen improvise one by crossing their swords and both Aimée and M. Jacques exchange the vows they would have taken before a priest. Aimée shows the true measure of herself in this scene full of a pathos heightened by the imminent death of Monsier Jacques. This fusion of love and death is a classic Barbey theme and the author draws our attention to it repeatedly, dwelling on the fact that death itself broke these solemn vows, insisting on Aimée's decision that her wedding-dress should become a shroud for M. Jacques. There is nothing morbid in all of this, but there is the tragic reminder that some cannot love with impunity, that love creates vulnerability.

After the recounting of the second expedition, the novel becomes an accumulation of incidents intended to produce surprise or shock. The reader learns of the stupefying torture inflicted by des Touches on the miller who betrayed him, des Touches' dramatic departure for England to resume his mission, and — several decades after the principal events of the story — Barbey's visit to des Touches in the insane asylum. The visit is recorded, not primarily because it occurred in reality, but because it offered one final opportunity to contrast the present with the past and also because it allowed Barbey to answer a question raised during the course of the novel. It had been known by those involved that Aimée de Spens would blush intensely whenever the Chevalier's name was spoken, but no one had ever determined why. During the course of his brief visit, Barbey is able to shake des Touches out of his insanity long enough to learn the reason for Aimée's mysterious reaction to his name. The Chevalier had once sought refuge from his enemies in Aimée's bedroom and as the soldiers of the Republic began to surround the house, preparing to enter — suspecting quite rightly that des Touches was within — Aimée began disrobing slowly near the window. Since her reputation for extreme propriety was well-known, the soldiers assumed that no man could possibly be present, promptly left the area and thus des Touches was spared a sure death. The experience was traumatic for Aimée who valued modesty very highly; she never recovered from the shock, and her face would turn flaming red whenever she heard the Chevalier's name. This is yet another instance of Barbey's interest in physiological and psychosomatic anomalies,[7] which is somewhat unusual for a writer long regarded as simply another Romantic.

X *Conclusion*

Le Chevalier des Touches constitutes something of an exception in Barbey's fiction, for here his obsession with the exceptional and the bizarre is attenuated in favor of heroism. The work is often referred to as a historical novel, but it would be inaccurate to place it in the same category as classics of the genre, Hugo's *Notre-Dame de Paris* or Flaubert's *Salammbô*. The genre requires considerable research, documentation and precise detail; but such demands exceed Barbey's temperament and resources. History was for him largely a refuge and a pretext for creative brooding. In this instance, the documentation is rudimentary, but adequate to allow a gifted novelist to recapture the manners, feelings and spirit of a vanished age, the atmosphere of a given moment in history. The fictionalized historical reality one finds here is not the reality of demonstrable fact, but rather a form of what Barbey himself called "l'idéalité" or what might have been. One does not regret the lack of detailed historical data, since this lack does not detract from the novel's effectiveness or power of evocation.

In both matter and manner Barbey gave proof of sound judgment, a trait also of the works still to be discussed. In choosing to relate one of the high points in the history of the Norman Chouans, in having the events retold by a participant instead of having them reconstructed directly by an omniscient narrator, Barbey succeeds remarkably well in contrasting what was and what is. Those who sit in the Touffedelys salon actively listening to Mlle de Percy have a lackluster present and an even less glamorous future, but they do have a memorable heroic past. The reconquest of the past, the recreation of a world that is no more, making the reader feel the *grandeur* or the poetry of the past — these are the strengths of the novel. Barbey is also pleading the case of memory and tradition in an increasingly forgetful world and is telling us that certain people, less superficial than others, remain forever scarred by the past. In addition, the rancor sometimes expressed here is that of Barbey the solitary spokesman for the disenfranchised nobility. He is also teaching us that exalting the past is an effective way of excoriating the present.

XI   Un prêtre marié

Written between 1854 and 1863, published in 1865, *Un prêtre marié* ("A Married Priest") is one of Barbey's most complex works and has many sources. He had long been fascinated by the idea of expiation, as developed by Joseph de Maistre, and more specifically by the theory that the innocent, through their sufferings, help atone for the sins of the guilty. At the same time, Barbey was influenced by his fiancée, Madame de Bouglon, for whom he tried to temper the violent tone of his writings. Calixte Sombreval, the daughter of the married priest, incarnates the idealism traceable in large part to Joseph de Maistre and Madame de Bouglon, while the married priest himself bears the diabolical imprint of some of Byron's characters.

With every novel he published, Barbey attracted increasingly wider notice, but the reviews were not necessarily the favorable ones he longed for. Zola, for example, while disagreeing with the ideas set forth in *Un prêtre marié,* was impressed by the work's strength and boldness, yet made a major interpretive error in assuming that it dealt with the question of the celibacy of the clergy, an issue much discussed during the eighteen-sixties. Others, recognizing the novel's rather appreciable power, expressed serious doubts about its greatness; and Léon Bloy's laudatory article did not appear until 1876.

Un prêtre marié relates the story of Jeam Sombreval who leaves the priesthood during the chaotic days of the French Revolution, marries and becomes a well-known chemist. After his wife's death, he returns to Normandy with his daughter Calixte, settling down at the Château du Quesnay, to the great scandal of the residents in the area who had known him as a priest. Upon learning these details about her father's background, Calixte, afflicted with a severe neu-

rosis, resolves to bring her father back to the faith and to the priesthood, while Sombreval devotes his prodigious energy to the hopeless task of finding a cure for his daughter. He eventually convinces
himself that she will be cured only if she agrees to marry Néel de
Néhou, a young nobleman who loves her passionately. In the face
of her obstinate refusal, he feigns a conversion and returns to the
clerical state; in his estimate, this will liberate her from her self-
imposed obligation to expiate her father's sins, and will end the
rumors about their incestuous relationship. When Calixte is made
aware that her father is living a sacrilege, she is horrified and dies
from an acute attack of tetanus. Having returned too late for his
daughter's burial, Sombreval is overcome by a superhuman rage at
having lost his *raison d'être,* and commits suicide by jumping into
the pond at le Quesnay, clutching her body in his arms.

Though the characters and the setting are Norman, one hesitates
to call this a regional novel, since the Normandy depicted here is
viewed through an obscuring and perturbing prism; the Château du
Quesnay is located in some remote corner of a Normandy distorted
by an author striving to deepen the darkness and the mystery
around his married priest. The pond at le Quesnay is compared to
the Orfano Canal in Venice, both being watery graves for
unremembered people — victims of either murder or suicide, no
one can be certain. Several of the secondary characters add much to
this disquieting atmosphere: la Malgaigne, an old sibyl endowed
with the eerie gift of accurate prophecy, and the two Negro servants
taken in by Sombreval, ignorant, superstitious, silent, terrifying to
the people of the countryside. The era is the same as in
L'Ensorcelée and *Le Chevalier des Touches,* an era characterized as
the end of a world, the illustrious families of the past having become extinct through excessive self-indulgence or because of the
Revolution. This whole nightmarish scene is an abomination of
desolation, with the Château, shaped like an enormous white sepul-
cher, isolated from the world outside, and the characters separated
from one another by irrefragable differences. Huysmans expressed
it well: "All the mysterious horror of the Middle Ages hovered over
this unlikely book, *A Married Priest;* magic was mixed with religion, occult learning with prayer and, more merciless, more savage
than the Devil, the God of original sin relentlessly tortured the
innocent Calixte, His reprobate . . ."[8]

Sombreval is a colossus, not unlike the Abbé de la Croix-Jugan in *L'Ensorcelée,* a man gifted with the qualities of a leader and deemed at one time to have a brilliant future in the Church. Having lost the faith, he chooses to leave the priesthood and studies chemistry, more specifically the formation and decomposition of the blood, becoming an associate of a celebrated chemist whose daughter he marries. His wife is traumatized when told that her husband is a former priest and dies upon giving birth to their child, Calixte. When the gravity of the latter's illness is recognized, Sombreval abandons all personal ambition and begins to exist solely as a father and a man of science, devoting his life to the quest of the right chemical formula capable of producing the medication which will cure Calixte:

... this combination [of the right chemical elements] might be for me what the structure of the diamond was for Lavoisier, a dream, a chimera, an impossibility, but it doesn't matter! I am determined to pursue it night and day without rest or respite, until my final hour of awareness and intelligence, until my last look, until I breathe my last, which I will do in my laboratory. (p. 1020)

These words indicate to what extent Sombreval bears the stamp of his creator: his resolution is absolute, irreversible. The words suggest too that he is lucid enough to suspect that he might be pursuing the Chimera and when he later states that "Science is the Sphinx" (p. 1022), he betrays his spiritual kinship with characters found in late nineteenth-century French literature — avatars of Romantic heroes — who also pursued some impossible dream and were on a perpetual quest for something new.

Calixte acts mainly as a foil to her father. Having been taught the essentials of Catholicism at a very young age, she has an all-consuming desire to bring her father back to the faith and to the priesthood. Dream-like, she is less of a woman than an apparition, a vision of an ethereal beauty. She lives in the odor of sanctity and combines the qualities of an angel in exile with those of the martyr: "Calixte suffered in her body and in her spirit: in her body she suffered because of her illness and in her spirit she suffered because of her father, but she was all the more beautiful for it. She had the Christian beauty, the double poetry, the double virtue of Innocence and Expiation..." (p. 920). She is loved by Néel de Néhou, a pale blond young man whose passion and strength give the lie to his womanly appearance. Little need be said concerning the secondary characters, such as Néel's fiancée, Bernardine de Lieusaint whose role is to be rejected by him, or the Abbé Méautis who decides that Calixte must be told at all cost that her father's return to the faith is insincere, hence sacrilegious.

XII *Transgression and Expiation*

The above should make it abundantly clear that *Un prêtre marié* is anything but a social novel; on the contrary, Barbey has created here a "no exit" situation, an infernal *huis-clos,* the only links existing between le Quesnay and the outside world being essentially negative, destructive. Witness for example the ugliness of the un-founded rumors about Sombreval's incestuous attachment to Calixte, resulting in his tragic decision to feign a return to the faith, or — even more negative — the Abbé Méautis' decision to reveal to Calixte the sacrilegious nature of her father's action. The relation-ships existing between the main characters are also destructive, for they are emotionally unbalanced in the extreme: Sombreval and Néel by their excessive futile love for Calixte, the latter by her intemperate and equally futile determination to "save" her father.

The further the reader progresses in the world of the novel, the more immersed he becomes in a world of sin and morbidity. Having rejected God, Sombreval is labeled a deicide (p. 891); be-cause Sombreval has left the priesthood and married, his father is fatally stricken, so that he is also a parricide (*ibid.*); for persisting in the path of unbelief, causing his daughter untold suffering, he is guilty of infanticide (p. 1067). In addition, Barbey holds him responsible for the death of his wife, who is traumatized when she hears that her husband is a priest and thereafter loses her will to live. More grievous in the eyes of the Church are blasphemy and sacrilege, sins committed repeatedly by Sombreval who reaches new heights of blasphemy at his daughter's grave (pp. 1218-19). From the very beginning, he is depicted as the quintessential sinner who seems incapable of anything but evil; his simulated return to the priesthood is a case in point. He does this to liberate Calixte from her self-imposed yoke, so that she will be free to marry Néel and find the happiness Sombreval wants for her; yet Barbey under-lines the effects of this decision on Néel: "The idea too of evil *in*

itself — of the *absolute* evil which Sombreval was about to commit
... and the certain damnation of this impenitent who was going to
drink and eat his eternal judgment every day with the bread and
wine of the holy chalice added religious terror to the young man's
human terror..." (p. 1112). The use of the terms "evil in itself,"
"absolute evil" indicates that for the author, the act represents the
ne plus ultra of what man can do when he resolves to defy God.
One of the most succinct and accurate interpretations of *Un prêtre
marié* has been offered by B. G. Rogers when he calls it "a work
devoted to the physical, even sensual description of sacrilege in all
its forms, a work whose theme, construction and originality all
spring from a violent fascination with blasphemy..."[9]

One may object however that Sombreval's lack of faith exon-
erates him and justifies his behavior; Barbey has taken this objec-
tion into account and has dealt with it explicitly in the structure of
the novel itself. In order to exploit fully the literary potential of
Sombreval's behavior, Barbey needed several characters sensitive
and aware enough to assess the enormity of these sins; virtually all
the characters serve this purpose, responding with horror to
Sombreval himself and to Calixte — that unspeakably monstrous
being who should never have been born, the daughter of a married
priest! After Calixte has prevailed upon her father to attend mass,
the reaction is described in these terms: "When they were seen
entering the church, indignation spread through the congregation,
which shuddered, ready to burst... On seeing Sombreval and his
daughter, everyone grasped their chairs, moving back a bit, as if
fearing contact with these infamous, plague-stricken beings..."
(p. 934). But sacrilege does not produce an over-reaction solely in
the popular imagination; the gravity of Sombreval's false conversion is the subject of considerable heart-wrenching thought by the
Abbé Méautis who finally concludes that the idea of mass being
celebrated by a non-believer is unbearable. That is why after much
prayer and meditation, knowing fully that the blow may be fatal to
her, the Abbé decides to reveal to Calixte the truth about the
horrendous imposture about to be perpetrated by her father. He
hopes that she will be able to make him change his mind. Risking
the life of a young woman is yet another means of allowing the
reader to measure the seriousness of sacrilege.

Condemned by a number of characters — sometimes amusingly,
as when he is called "a real Nebuchadnezzar of vices" (p. 1050) —

ostracized by nearly everyone, what is Sombreval's attitude toward his own acts? Since he is genuinely a nonbeliever, can he legitimately be held responsible for his apostasy, his sacrilegious acts, his blasphemous words? The answer would have to be a qualified yes. According to traditional Church teachings, which Barbey accepted, a man ordained to the priesthood is a priest forever and his soul forever bears a sacred imprint setting him apart from all men, despite the vagaries of his personal feelings or beliefs. The modern reader, however, is not likely to judge Sombreval a monster, given the man's total sincerity and his selfless love for his daughter. There can be no doubt that his conduct is that of an authentic nonbeliever, as proven by his every word, deed, thought and feeling, none so moving perhaps as the avowal of his futile prayers to preserve his faith, of his supplications to God to deliver him from doubt (p. 1015).

Un prêtre marié belongs to a Catholic tradition which today may well appear archaic, but which had obtained since the Middle Ages, lasting well into the twentieth century. Apostasy and sacrilege were thought to be the work of the Devil, who took many forms, having at his disposal a variety of means to lure man away from God. The discussion of previous works has made manifest Barbey's obsession with Satan, usually in relation to forbidden love. Sombreval is a Satan-figure in the minds of those around him, in part because he is that unthinkable being, a married priest — though that in itself would qualify him for the role — but perhaps to a greater extent because he is a man of science. The point is well exemplified when the Abbé Méautis visits Sombreval in his laboratory, feeling as if he were in the antechamber of Hell:

The retorts, stills, Volta cells standing in every part of the room, the countless aparatus looking like weapons loaded, stuffed, ready to burst, to vomit death; the strange containers, the outrageous vases with fantastic lines and contours — bronze or crystal chimeras — some with long necks stretched out or drawn in like serpents, others with bulging bellies of pregnant beasts about to give birth — all of that appeared to him like an immobile but threatening menagerie of animals from another world momentarily congealed by a supreme power, but apocalyptically hideous (p. 1078).

The laboratory seen for the first time by an unsophisticated country priest illustrates on a minor scale what Sombreval represents for his neighbors. Dwelling amidst people for whom Satan is beyond all reasonable doubt a living reality, Sombreval is feared, maligned, insulted and spurned. That he is not a willful embodiment of Satan or an evil force in himself does not make him less fascinating to the modern reader whose world-view is perforce different from that of nineteenth-century Normans.

Through Sombreval, Barbey also develops the related theme of eternal damnation, leaving no doubt in our minds that such is the destiny of both Sombreval and Calixte; for at the moment of death, in reference to her father and herself, Calixte says: "*We* are doomed!" (p. 1201). She thus concedes defeat, recognizing the futility of all the superhuman efforts she has made to save both her father and herself. Any subsisting doubt in the reader's mind regarding the possibility of salvation is eliminated by the final paragraph which states that after his death, Sombreval has indeed been damned.

It is difficult not to see in such an obsession, beyond the Jansenism of which it is a manifestation, a yielding to the grimmest kind of pessimism and the most despairing expression of the question "Ad quid?" Must one go further yet and see the compulsion to damn Sombreval one of the most frantic forms of Barbey's sadism? The question has no conclusive answer, but personally I would interpret this obsession with damnation as the need to probe more deeply the realm of the forbidden, and to contemplate its consequences. In most of his fiction, Barbey has striven to show "the underside of the cards" of purely human situations, hence it seems plausible that just for once, Barbey the impatient, the impulsive, wanted to allow himself an incursion into the afterlife to evoke the underside of God's cards.

While the novel betrays a fascination with damnation, a similar fascination is obvious regarding the futile attempts made by Calixte to expiate her father's sins. The recounting of these attempts is unique in all of Barbey's work, for it combines, to a degree never attained, either before or after that novel, a certain kind of mysticism and a sometimes clinical description of an illness remarkable for its complexity and its originality. The first sign of this illness is a cross imprinted on the child's forehead, a mark sometimes found weakly imprinted on infants at birth. But here the sign is interpreted as a reminder of the Cross betrayed by Sombreval; the mark is permanent and Calixte will discreetly cover it with a scarlet head-band.

"Neurosis" is the term most frequently used by Barbey in reference to this illness, a deliberately vague term alluding to a condition which had mystified Europe's most celebrated medical men. According to Sombreval, its origins are pre-natal and psycho-somatic, a consequence of the discovery, on the part of Calixte's mother, that she had unknowingly married a defrocked priest. There are several scenes describing symptoms in considerable detail, when the girl is shown, for example, walking during a seizure, with eyes rolled back, foaming at the mouth, yet remaining lucid enough not to fall or to hurt herself (pp. 1018–19). Prolonged fainting spells alternate with convulsions and sleep-walking without forewarning; but the vivid realism of these descriptions has not been adequately appreciated, probably because these elements are less evident, less spectacular than sacrilege, blasphemy or the non-celibacy of a priest.[10]

Even more curious than the physiological dimension of this illness is its religious or mystical dimension, though in the novel itself, the two are not separable. This latter point is well illustrated by a hallucination which precedes a seizure. Standing before a crucifix, Calixte sees blood:

Lord God! she said, it *is* blood! — liquid blood— real blood coming from your wounds, oh! my Savior! Horrors! Such a thing had not been seen for so long; bleeding crucifixes will be seen again! Formerly ... in the ancient days .. when they bled, people used to say that it was against some great sinner in hiding ... and that the angry blood of the Lord was gushing forth against him to denounce his presence to all men... But who is the guilty one here, oh God Whom I love, for Your blood to gush against me with such force! (p. 1140)

Stepping back to move away from this blood, she grasps her head then shrieks when she feels blood flowing from the cross on her forehead. This mixture of bloody mysticism and medical observations recurs frequently until her death, betraying Barbey's fascination with goriness and morbidity, but this is also related to the long tradition of martyrs and saints bearing stigmata, i.e. wounds resembling those of the crucified Christ.

Underlying all of this fascination with sin and damnation there is also what Barbey called "the great Christian idea of Expiation,"[11] one of the novel's main themes, the atonement of Sombreval's sins through the suffering of Calixte. From the standpoint of orthodox Catholicism, the idea of expiation is of course perfectly valid in principle; and one might even state further that in choosing a mental illness or neurosis as a means of atonement, Barbey made a sound decision if one bears in mind the old custom of exorcising mentally ill people thought to have been possessed by the devil. It should be said, in all fairness, that Barbey's Catholicism as expressed in this novel seems unduly harsh, destructive and negativistic; the austere, forbidding God of justice and punishment was better suited to Barbey's temperament and world-view than the God of clemency and mercy. Furthermore, while the ideas of expiation and of solidarity among Catholics are indeed orthodox Catholic doctrines, the Church does not teach that the sufferings of a certain person are necessarily intended to atone for the sins of another; this degree of specificity in the interpretation of an individual's destiny belongs to Barbey alone. Thus, one is tempted to say that Barbey has created his own form of Catholicism, but that is true only to the extent that he has exaggerated or modified certain aspects of an existing religion. A considerable distance separates Barbey's religious views, largely Jansenistic, from Huysmans' esthetic Catholicism, for example — the latter constituting a much more pronounced departure from the more familiar teachings of the Roman Church. Barbey's religion is characterized by an obsession with sin, damnation, hell, and the enormous difficulty of eternal salvation.

Yet, in *Un prêtre marié* much more than in any other novel by Barbey, one senses the appeal of salvation, of heaven, and faith in the afterlife. We find here a co-existence of two phenomena: nostalgia for the eternal bliss promised those who achieve salvation and fascination with the man who, while having the temerity of denying the existence of the afterlife, creates for himself the worst possible fate, eternal damnation. Barbey may condemn, as indeed he does more than once, the behavior of Sombreval, but Sombreval constantly enthralls him, and in fact Barbey becomes quite explicit when he refers to him as "ce sublime horrible" (p. 1108) or again when he alludes to Sombreval's "satanically magnanimous design" (p. 1149). Sombreval combines several of Barbey's obsessions: as a priest, he is a sacred being and almost as mysterious as woman; as a strong-willed individualist who rebels against "the system," and damns himself in the process, he assumes the qualities of a Judas, committing the ultimate transgression, a sin so heinous that even his daughter's unutterable suffering cannot expiate it.

XIII *Love, Violence and Death*

Love moves the main characters to perform some rather innovative acts of violence, several instances of which are set forth with a gusto for macabre realism. After feigning his return to the faith out of love for his daughter, Sombreval must spend some time in a monastery to atone for his sins and to demonstrate his sincerity; he goes about achieving these goals with a passion which Barbey the extremist could not help admiring: "To expiate the crimes of his life, he underwent extraordinary macerations. Eating only bread and water, he wore a hair-shirt and it was even said that under his hair-shirt he wore an iron belt armed with a spike which, under the pressure of a spring, penetrated his side and remained there" (p. 1167). Those around him shuddered from the frightful sounds they heard when he was flogging himself, and thus Barbey combines, in this complex thematic network, paternal love, sacrilege, the theme of the mask along with a note of masochism.

Equally innovative is Néel's flirtation with suicide, carried out in order to convince Calixte of his love for her. In a carriage drawn by two untamed horses, he wanders erratically about the countryside, leaving havoc and destruction in his wake, heading generally for the Château de Quesnay where he will be delivered alive or dead, having proved that he is ready to risk everything, even his life, to win the hand of his beloved. It is an extreme, somewhat gratuitous way of making a point; and aside from the wild romanticism of the act, its esthetic aspects are worth noting: "He prepared for himself a magnificent suicide with the art and coquetry of a Sardanapalus. He played everything with this sparkling card — the magic of a superb danger!" (p. 1024). The carriage has the gracefulness of an ancient chariot, the headstall is adorned with tufts of pink ribbon and Néel is wearing his holiday garb — in short, he sets out to court death with the accoutrement of a dandy. The gesture is futile inasmuch as it procures for him neither love nor death, but simply the destruction of two excellent horses.

Love, violence and death are brought together in a manner even more far-fetched after the death of Calixte. In order to ascertain that she is really dead and not in one of her deeper trances, Néel takes the red-hot poker from the fireplaces, drives it into her foot to begin desperately burning "the beautiful insensitive feet which the fire consumed.... Executioner out of tenderness, he became drunk over this action mixed with horror and determination" (p. 1205). When there is no sign of life, Néel, broken by despair, is compelled to admit that his beloved is indeed dead. Despite Barbey's disclaimer that this is merely an old peasant custom, it is difficult not to see the act's sexual, even sadistic overtones. By far the boldest association of love and death occurs in one of the final scenes where Sombreval howls with powerless rage and disinters Calixte's body: "With his forehead, his lips, his entire face, Sombreval convulsively furrowed the body he held and was lifting in his arms. He thrust his head into the lap of his dear dead daughter — with the fury of a feeling which knows it is powerless..." while Néel stands by, jealous of Sombreval's macabre self-indulgence (p. 1217).

It is a fitting end to a liaison characterized from the very beginning by a pronounced association with death. Very soon, Néel found "charming, melodious harmonies between this ravishing creature, so ill yet so young, and a certain country cemetery surrounded by hawthornes in bloom, dotted with daisies, where pigeons ... would fly away like souls, from the grass around the tombstones" (p. 936). The association is of course highly subjective yet it does point up the melancholy, painful, mournful aspects of human love and its transitory quality as well; the association was well known to Baudelaire, for one finds many variations of this theme in *Fleurs du Mal*. The theme is taken up again and again throughout the novel, with Néel telling Calixte "...if you die, I must die. We will drink death from the same glass, and never will I have drunk anything better than this death which you make me love" (p. 992).

One might be tempted to dismiss such passages as purely conventional romanticism, a pastiche perhaps, of pages written by Lamartine or Musset, but there is no doubting the felt quality of such statements made by a young man who accurately senses the imminence of death: "...allow me to call you my fiancée! And be my fiancée for what little time we have left to live, until we share the same grave!" (p. 993). The feeling is so genuine, so persistent that at the end of the novel, the author convincingly writes the following words about Néel: "He had created for himself a kind of poetry from the idea of dying with her, and he missed this poetry. In his love, this was the only selfishness left" (pp. 1154–55). The most powerful expression of the theme is reserved for la Malgaigne, the sinister prophetess who *sees* that Néel is aware of Sombreval's imposture, that the young man is an accomplice in the perpetration of a sacrilegious fraud and that upon this fraud rests his hope of marrying Calixte. Prophesying the death of Calixte and Néel both, she states tersely: "You were betrothed at the black altar and you will be married in the earth" (p. 1115), thus making explicit the links between love, death and irremediable evil.

XIV *Conclusion*

The discussion of these four novels indicates that Barbey had a painful awareness of each individual's solitude, a tragic sense of *l'amour impossible* or the essential inability of men and women to achieve significant and lasting communication. Yet, thrashing in the coils of this isolation, human beings do make the attempt to break out of a seemingly metaphysical imprisonment within the self, encountering every manner of obstacle until death puts an end to striving. Variations on the related themes of striving and failure are constants in Barbey's works; it sometimes seems as if all his considerable talents, his sense of observation, his fertile imagination, his sound intuitive sense, had been mobilized to suggest that for reasons without number, human beings simply cannot break out of their essential solitude. This thoroughgoing despair about love, the all-pervasive sense of the sterility of passion, the destructiveness of certain characters, the premature death of young people without offspring — all of these elements, set agains the apocalyptic backdrop of the Revolution, constitute the stark "end of a world" atmosphere which prevails throughout these novels and stories. Yet none of this morbidity detracts from Barbey's esthetic triumph over the forces of darkness.

CHAPTER 4

Erotic Horrors:
From Les Diaboliques (1874)
to Ce qui ne meurt pas (1883)

THROUGHOUT his life Barbey had been obsessed with passion, eroticism, violence, transgression, and death. These
obsessions did not abate in his later years; for, at least in the *Diaboliques,* they found a masterful aesthetic expression. The matter
of reconciling such concerns with Barbey's Catholicism is admittedly troublesome, as he himself recognized in his Preface to the
Diaboliques: "Obviously, with the title *Les Diaboliques,* these
stories do not pretend to be a book of prayers or an *Imitation of
Christ* . . . yet they are the work of a Christian moralist, but of one
who prides himself on truthful though very bold observation, and
who believes that powerful artists can portray anything at all and
that their portrayal is always moral enough when it is tragic and
when it provides a sense of the horror of what is portrayed."[1] The
foregoing might well have served as a Preface to all his fictional
works, and one is tempted to agree with the arguments he advances. Yet his fascination with sin and the ease with which he con-
jures up erotic nightmares leave one skeptical. Obviously, the
Catholic writer is free to portray the many forms of sin, but one
does not sense, in the works of other Catholic writers, the same
degree of fascination, the same absence of revulsion, that one
recognizes in Barbey's stories. The issue has no satisfactory resolution, and it is raised only because of its relative historical importance. Twentieth-century readers will judge these works solely on
aesthetic grounds; and here one need not equivocate, for they are
assuredly quite deserving of our attention.

I   Les Diaboliques

Les Diaboliques, that extraordinary collection of six novellas, appeared in 1874 and remains Barbey's masterpiece. The humiliating trial caused by its publication has been discussed in the first chapter of the present work; its net effect was to perplex even more the author's contemporaries, already puzzled by his paradoxical nature. While the book did not receive the acclaim it deserved, it did enhance his reputation among a growing number of admirers; and it secured his niche in literary history.

The extensive range of his readings, including memoirs, regional history, medical treatises, the works of Sade and countless other works, has made it impossible to identify the sources of these stories with any certainty. Also, the anecdotes heard during his childhood and youth made lasting impressions upon him and doubtless contributed certain elements to plot, character or setting. Obviously, the following discussion of the *Diaboliques,* because of its briefness, cannot do the work full justice; and, as often as possible, I have let the author speak in his own words so that the reader might obtain a more accurate idea of the quality of the work.

II   *"Le rideau cramoisi"*

As a seventeen-year-old sub-lieutenant, the future Vicomte de Brassard is assigned to a small garrison in a remote part of Normandy. The boredom of this cheerless assignment is relieved only by the headiness of wearing a uniform for the first time and the hope of going into battle soon. Given the total lack of a social life, there is no chance of meeting any young ladies *comme il faut;* and Brassard, residing in the home of a nondescript older couple, is astounded one day when Alberte, the couple's daughter — whose existence he had not suspected — suddenly returns home to stay. After one uneventful month during which Alberte remains totally impassive, she inexplicably grasps Brassard's hand under the dinner table. Concealing his shock with great difficulty, he is overcome with pleasure; and later that evening he writes her an impassioned note which he delivers on the following day. Her silence, lasting for another interminable month, leaves him craving for her desperately; his exacerbated yearning finally ends on the night she visits his room and becomes his mistress. She returns every other night for six months until she dies in his arms while making love. Panic-stricken by her death, by the possibility that he might be partly to blame and by the thought of her parents discovering this horrible scandal, he rushes to the commanding officer who orders him to leave town on the next coach and subsequently arranges to have him transferred. Nothing is ever learned about the reactions of Alberte's parents or the probable disgrace brought upon the family by Brassard's violation of the code of hospitality.

The Vicomte de Brassard who relates the story to Barbey obviously fascinates the author. Before hearing the tale, Barbey has already met him socially and can therefore provide enough information about his past to make him captivating. An old beau with the poetry of the soldier about him, he was for Barbey "a formidable jolly fellow who, I thought, was lined with copper like a Greek brig" (p. 24), a real sixteenth-century type of colossus, facetious, jocund, exuberant. From his tailor-made glass of Bohemian crystal, he would drink a full bottle of Bordeaux at one go — like a Pole, Barbey specifies (p. 16). A Knight of Malta, he still wears his ribbon on occasion, out of foppishness, even though the Order was abolished by the Revolution. He also symbolizes the twilight of an age: "This setting sun of a grandiose elegance so long radiant would have made all those stylish little crescents now on the horizon seem thin and wan" (p. 17).

As a young army officer, the Vicomte was also a dandy and hence placed his own pride and independence above the authority of his superiors. Disdainful of discipline, he was frequently absent without leave, yet careful to report for duty whenever his company stood guard at the Tuileries, since the Duchesse d'Angoulême always had a few gracious words for him. This latter fact did not escape the notice of the Minister, who would gladly have promoted him, but with his persistent insubordination, he was fortunate to be spared a court-martial. Once, on the parade-ground, he had even drawn his sword against the inspector general because of some mild criticism. In the field, however, he took his duties quite seriously. In all circumstances he was highly respected by his men, perhaps because he encouraged duels among them as the best means he knew to develop the military spirit, and rewarded the winners of these duels with anything apt to spruce up their uniforms. He thus appealed to their conceit and affectation, and in return they adored him, striving to be as brave, punctilious and coquettish as he demanded, thereby embodying the type of the old French soldier. During the Revolution of 1830, he successfully carried out an extremely hazardous mission, demonstrating his value as an officer and his worth as a true nobleman.

By now the reader is well-acquainted with Barbey's penchant for exceptional characters, but in the portrait-gallery created by Barbey, the Vicomte de Brassard is particularly memorable for combining dandyism, effective military leadership, and, even as an army officer, the ability to apply the well-known French *esprit critique* to the army, to an institution one is prone to take quite seriously. He also has a touch of the poet, referring to the young ladies of the town as "dreams hidden . . . beneath veils, glimpsed at from afar" (p. 27). When he speaks about the anticipation of his first battle and living for that moment, one hears echoes of the French *moraliste:* ". . . one lives more in the life one doesn't have than in the life one does have. My self-worth was based on what I would be in the future, just like the miser, and I understood very well those devout persons who manage in this life like one manages in a death-trap in which one has only to spend a night. Nothing resembles a monk more than a soldier, and I was a soldier!" (p. 28).

At the end of "Le rideau cramoisi," Alberte is scarcely less of an enigma than she is at the outset. When Brassard first sees her, she has the attitude of an archduchess, neither scorn nor disdain, but an infuriating impassiveness which says, "For me you do not exist" (p. 31). She is compared to Velasquez' "Infanta with Spaniel," and until she squeezes Brassard's hand, we learn nothing else about her, except that she is a quiet, proper eighteen-year-old. Thus the Vicomte is thunder-struck by her unexpected provocativeness which betrays the extraordinary ease with which she can pretend that nothing untoward is taking place. There is something of the dandy in the remarkable self-assurance she displays during and after this incident, in her prodigious aplomb, her full and unflagging command of a situation she has created. On her first visit to Brassard's room, we are told that "her princess-like traits had not changed. They still had the immobility and the firmness of a medal" (p. 45). The mask of impassivity fits her as well as it would a dandy, and she has too the dandy's ability to shock (without ever betraying one's own feelings); but above all she has the dandy's self-possession. Yet the sum total of these distinctively male charac-

teristics does not detract from her essential feminity or voluptuousness.

Sphinx, vampire, *femme fatale,* she has the moral strength commonly associated with men. It is she who takes the initiative at the
dinner-table and it is she who crosses her parents' bedroom to visit
Brassard. Every other night, she risks discovery and disgrace by tip-
toeing to her rendez-vous, taking the same risks, of course, by
remaining there as long as she likes. After making love, both lie
still, in mortal dread of being discovered, as Brassard recalls: "It
was intoxicating and sobering at the same time, but it was terrible!" (p. 46). The themes of danger and secrecy related to passion
are well developed throughout the story; indeed, as the preceding
chapters have shown, they are obsessive themes in Barbey, justifying the phrase "an esthetic of surprise" applied to his work. These
obsessions are verbalized by the Vicomte de Brassard, but the voice
is Barbey's own: "I understood the happiness of those who hide. I
understood the enjoyment of mystery in complicity, which, even
without the hope of success, would still produce incorrigible con-
spirators" (p. 48). These feelings are expressed perhaps even more
felicitously by the image of making love on the blade of a saber laid
across an abyss. Yet throughout their liaison, Alberte maintains almost a perfect silence, uttering an occasional monosyllable in
response to Brassard's probing questions, remaining to the very
end a mystery woman apparently moved only by the formic acid of
lust.

More than thirty years later, Brassard recalls with a shudder the
immediate effects which her death had upon him, and the horror he
felt is powerfully evoked. The physical hand of fear upon his head,
his hair turning to needles, his spine melting into icy mud, his hallu-
cinations, all of these sensations are recalled in vivid detail, as are
his futile attempts to find an adequate solution: "I had the strength
to take Alberte's body and, lifting it by the arms, placed it on my
shoulders. A horrible cope, much heavier than that of the damned
in Dante's Hell! One has to have carried, as I did, this cope of flesh
which an hour before had made my blood boil with desire and
which now was betraying me! ... One has to have carried it in
order to know what it was!" (p. 53). But he gives up on this impossible effort to place Alberte back in her own bed and finally,
without finding a means of saving her from disgrace, he places himself at his Colonel's mercy. The mystery of death in a lover's arms

remains intact, muffled, silent except for the guilt which has plagued Brassard through the years. As in previous stories, the association of death and passion is well established, the cause and effect relationship between them being perhaps less equivocal.

"Le rideau cramoisi" is a tale within a tale. Brassard relates the story to Barbey during a layover in the same little town where the events took place. The coach in which they are sharing a compartment breaks down just a few feet from the house where Brassard was traumatized by his horrifying experience with Alberte. Choosing this setting for the narration might appear capricious, but Barbey's need to find or to create links between past and present is well-known. From the coach, the interlocutor can see the same crimson curtain (or an exact duplicate) which hung in Brassard's room some thirty years before. The image of the crimson curtain is well chosen. Its overtones of concealment and mystery are well suited to arouse anyone's curiosity, while the crimson evokes passion, blood and, by extension, death.

The mood is set early in the story, before the narrative begins, when Barbey sets forth the impressions of a traveler crossing villages and towns by night, musing on the possible reasons why, here and there, a window is lit. That someone should be awake while the rest of the world sleeps is in itself quite imposing, he says. "But not knowing what is keeping someone awake behind a window with drawn curtains, where a light indicates life and thought, adds the poetry of dream to the poetry of reality" (p. 19). An ironic note is added during the description of the broken-down coach: "Our sleeping coach resembled an enchanted carriage, rooted to the spot by the fairies' wand, at some crossroads, in the forest of Sleeping Beauty" (p. 22). The irony becomes obvious if we consider that the story can indeed be read as a cruel variation of the Sleeping Beauty legend. The story closes on a note of greater mystery when Brassard briefly glimpses the profile of a slender woman behind the crimson curtain: "'Alberte's shadow, said the Captain. Chance is much too mocking tonight,' he added with bitterness" (p.57).

III   *"Le plus bel amour de Don Juan"*

The narration of the main events takes place in the boudoir of the Comtesse de Chiffrevas in the elegant Faubourg Saint-Germain. The occasion is an elaborate dinner-party given by twelve prominent ladies of the *noble faubourg,* former mistresses of the Comte Jules-Amédée-Hector Ravila de Ravilès, a Parisian Don Juan. The multi-course meal which takes place in an atmosphere of sparkling wit, verve, and brio, lasts until dawn when the Comte is asked to relate the story of the conquest which most flattered his pride and which he considers — at the end of his long career — to have been his finest love. He begins with a detailed portrait of an unnamed woman with whom he once had a relationship in Italy. Superlatives abound in his description of her; and just as his listeners become wary of such banal romanticism, he shifts the narrative focus to the woman's thirteen-year-old daughter who detested him intensely, avoiding him, fleeing his presence at every opportunity. A short while later, at her request, the girl's confessor reveals to her mother that she is pregnant. Horrified, the mother questions her at length about the circumstances of her pregnancy, thereby learning that one evening the girl sat in the arm-chair from which the Comte had just arisen and had the sensation of having fallen into fire, with the added feeling — it is a certainty in her mind — that she was pregnant. Such, in his opinion, is the finest love the Comte had ever inspired.

In many ways, it is a characteristic Barbey performance: the snobbery, the sexual oddity, the melancholy mood are again combined in the elaboration of a successful, if not masterful production. One is surprised that Barbey does not make greater use of the Don Juan legend itself in this piece, and the surprise ending would make the story appear insulting to the great legend, unless it were given a very precise interpretation, as will be seen.

The atmosphere is one of mellowed sensuality, and in Barbey's works sensuality is virtually synonymous with evil. The women around the Comte are women with whom he has had forbidden relationships, and the locale (the boudoir of a Countess) was expressly chosen because the boudoir had been the scene of his triumphs. They are clearly unrepentant women, since the occasion "was memory, regret, almost despair, but despair in full dress, concealed beneath smiles or laughter, yet still craving this feast, this last fling, this final escapade back to youth, this one final spree, after which it would be over forever!" (p. 63). The story is obviously a variation on the theme of the repentant sinner; far from being sorry for their sins, these women wish to honor the memory of these sins, regretful that they cannot be repeated, mourning the passing of their sinful youth, so that despite the tone of levity in evidence throughout most of the story, one can presume that these women too are "diabolical" and that — in line with Barbey's theological convictions — they will be damned to hell forever. Thus an atmosphere of sin begins to develop, but in the most sumptuous setting, amidst the splendor of crystals, candelabra and flowers; the scene is depicted as "a masterpiece of taste, refinement, patrician luxury, studied refinement and pretty ideas . . ." (*Ibid.*). To all of this Barbey adds a series of superlatives to evoke the charm, the daintiness, the headiness and especially the originality of the feast.

This rather unique feast is not unworthy of Don Juan, a member of "that ancient, eternal race of Juan, to whom God did not give the world, but allowed the devil to do so" (p. 61). Surrounded by twelve women à la Rubens, the Don's pride has been offered the perfect setting — a diabolically splendorous Last Supper — in which to share the story of his finest love. His narrative, though brief, is executed with the sparkle and verbal elegance one might expect. He also shows the keen psychological sense associated with his name, as when he differs with the "moralistes" who state that one's greatest love is neither the first nor the last, as many people believe, but rather the second: "But in matters of love, everything is true and everything is false..." (p. 68).

He shows the same competence when he speaks about the need to practice, in any amorous relationship, the great *art* of love which prevents love from dying. Such is the one flaw in his otherwise perfect Italian mistress: "She was certainly in love; but she lacked the art of love... She was the opposite of so many women who have the art but not the feeling! In order to understand and apply the policies of *The Prince,* one must already be a Borgia. Borgia precedes Machiavelli; one is the poet, the other the critic" (p. 70). That he taught her the art of love goes without saying, but to abstain from citing his mode of expression would do Barbey a grave injustice. The woman had loved once before, but platonically, hence after the fashion of a "white mass" said by young priests as an exercise, a preparation for the real mass: "When I entered her life, she was still at the stage of the white mass. I was her real mass, and she celebrated this mass with all the appropriate ceremonies, and she did it sumptuously, as would a cardinal" (p. 69). It should be noted that Barbey does nothing to attenuate the note of mild blasphemy in Don Juan's expression, and the absence of any condemnation whatever confirms our suspicion that he is a willing accomplice of this character who bears his own given name, Jules-Amédée.

The ugly thirteen-year-old daughter of this cardinal-like mistress experiences an almost convulsive horror whenever she sees Don Juan, acting (albeit not very effectively) as her mother's conscience, particularly since she has " a somber, Spanish, medieval, superstitious" kind of piety (p. 73). But again, this is merely the surface reality; for, as the climax indicates, the girl is actually struggling against an irresistible attraction. "Le plus bel amour de Don Juan" has often been dismissed as one of Barbey's weakest works; yet Jacques Petit's interpretation of the story as the youngster's discovery of evil is most convincing (p. 1307) and gives the work a much deeper meaning than that provided by previous critics. One might go further and see here an instance of evil's triumph over good. For the text makes it abundantly clear that the girl has struggled prodigiously to counter the Comte's appeal and that his non-physical seduction, followed by what she sincerely believes to be pregnancy, has taken place against her will. Having sat in the chair just vacated by the Comte, she was overcome by the warmth of his recent presence there, her will was broken, and she experienced the same psychosomatic effects she would have felt if she had indeed conceived a child by him. Viewed in this light, the story is a tribute to the power of evil and is not unworthy of the Don Juan legend.

IV   *"Le bonheur dans le crime"*

While strolling through the Jardin des Plantes in the company of his friend, Doctor Torty, Barbey pauses before the cage of the black panther, admiring the animal's suppleness and power. The two men are struck by a phenomenally handsome couple, totally absorbed in one another, oblivious of their surroundings, the Comte and Madame Serlon de Savigny. Intrigued by the couple's extraordinary self-sufficiency and by the doctor's caustic remarks, Barbey prevails upon Torty to tell him the story of these two superior individuals. A quarter century before the scene just described, the young Hauteclaire Stassin, having learned her father's profession, had been giving fencing lessons in the Norman town of Valognes. The Comte Serlon de Savigny took lessons from Hauteclaire, a gifted and brilliant fencer, who had disappeared one day without a trace, after becoming the pride of the town. Called to visit the gravely ill Comtesse de Savigny, Dr. Torty discovered that Hauteclaire had become her servant. The Comtesse seemed unaware of the private relationship existing between Hauteclaire and the Comte. Shortly afterward, the doctor was urgently summoned to the Château de Savigny where the Comtesse had been poisoned by Hauteclaire. Knowing the complete truth about the cause of her death, the Comtesse obtained from the doctor a solemn assurance that he would not tarnish the family name by revealing the horrible truth. After the official two-year mourning period, Serlon married Hauteclaire, totally indifferent to the scandal-mongering he had caused and caring not one iota about marrying someone far beneath his social status. Together, Hauteclaire and Serlon form a self-contained world, neither one ever showing a twinge of remorse.

Barbey paints a remarkable portrait of Dr. Torty, the man who played a key role in the events he relates. One suspects that Torty is a projection of the author and that Barbey attributes to him some of the outrageous statements he could not make in his own name because of his Catholicism. The reader's first impression is that of being in the presence of a thoroughgoing cynic with little or no real interest in human situations. Referring to his patients' attitude during his medical practice in Normandy, he says: "They had ... a choice to make between me and Extreme Unction and, pious though they were, they still chose me over the Holy Oils" (p. 82). His medical philosophy was that of Cabanis, i.e., absolute materialism, which was rather bold at the time. He had been a Leatherstocking on horseback, and had observed human beings too closely not to be a misanthrope. When Barbey expresses shock upon learning the true identity of the second Comtesse de Savigny, Torty calmly replies that one must not look too closely at anyone's origins. Yet Torty's curiosity proved almost overpowering when he discovered that Hauteclaire had entered Savigny's household as a servant to the Comtesse: "Ah! the pleasures of the observer! I would be able to indulge in the impersonal solitary pleasures of the observer, which I had always placed above all other pleasures..." (p. 103). His exacerbated curiosity transforms his "observation" into espionage, which is simply "observation at any cost" (p. 110) and which seems a form of voyeurism.

Having free access to the Savigny Château in his capacity as the family physician, he is able to observe very closely and to share with Barbey — a quarter of a century later — his understanding of the feelings involved in the *ménage à trois,* including Savigny's imprudence. Certain passions are born of imprudence, the observer states, and they would not exist without an element of danger. He cites the example of the sixteenth-century, an extremely passionate age, when the most magnificent cause of love was the very danger of love. A man consistently ran the risk of being stabbed or poisoned by his mistress's husband; yet, far from preventing forbidden love, danger merely provoked it. The same psychological laws obtained in the nineteenth century:

In our insipid modern mores in which law has replaced passion, it is obvious that the article of the Code applying to the husband guilty of having . . . introduced "a concubine into the conjugal residence," constitutes a rather ignoble danger. But for noble souls, precisely because it is ignoble, this danger is all the greater; and Savigny, by exposing himself to it, may have found the sole anxiety-ridden pleasure capable of intoxicating strong individuals (p. 105).

The words are spoken by Torty, but with considerable precision they express ideas and situations which recur repeatedly in Barbey's writings.

The reader's curiosity is aroused by the initial presentation of the couple at the Jardin des Plantes, just outside the cage of the Javanese panther, so supple, powerful and disdainful that the beast is superior to the spectators, until the chance arrival of Savigny and Hauteclaire: ". . . the woman, the unknown one, was like a human panther set before the animal panther, which she eclipsed . . ." (p. 86). In order to convince the animal of her superiority, Hauteclaire removes her glove, swats the panther's snout and withdraws her hand quickly enough to avoid the lightning-like bite of the beast. The Comte and Hauteclaire together form a true master-couple. Patrician, haughty, the Comte has a bearing which would have monopolized attention, were it not for Hauteclaire. The latter, dressed in black satin, resembles the great black Isis of the Musée Egyptien — stately, physically well endowed, exuding strength and a mysterious pride.

Mystery and masks had always been essential aspects of Hauteclaire Stassin. As a girl in Valognes, she kept her face concealed behind her fencing-mask or beneath the tightly laced black veil she

wore at Sunday mass. From the outset, she is clearly stronger than
Savigny, though the latter is far from being a weakling. She has the
strength of steel, and in the Middle Ages she would probably have
enjoyed wearing armor. Her unparalleled speed, grace and precision make of her an extraordinary fencer, so that during their first
match she defeats the Comte handily, without his touching her even
once. His initial impression of her is worth noting: "He found her
to be what she was, — a remarkable young lady, piquant and devil-
ishly provocative in her knitted silk hose, which set off a shape like
that of a Pallus of Velletri, and in her tight-fitting black morocco
jacket which accentuated a lusty, vigorous figure..." (p. 95). The
impression is most accurate, for her esthetic appeal is indeed exceptional; she and Savigny embracing by moonlight remind Torty of
the "groupe de Canova" so justly famous. In addition, she has the
qualities of a superb female animal, which are best conjured up by
the term "feminality."

The first Comtesse de Savigny belongs to a dying breed,
"exhausted, elegant, distinguished, haughty and who, from the
depths of their paleness and thinness, seem to say: 'I have been vanquished by time, like my race; I am dying, but I have only scorn for
you!'" (p. 101). She was born, it seems, to be victimized by a
woman like Hauteclaire, whom one might dismiss as a vulgar
opportunist, but for the excellent use she makes of her spectacular
gifts, as indicated above. Much to Barbey's chagrin, the new order
is clearly replacing the old, and rather ruthlessly so, as we have seen
in novel after novel. Here, however, Barbey attenuates the un-
pleasantness of this social change by making of Hauteclaire a superior being. Women like the Comtesse de Savigny are dying off,
overwhelmed by historical forces and the vices of their husbands;
but the Comtesse dies like the authentic noblewoman she truly is.
Knowing she has been poisoned by her servant, her husband's mistress, she shares this knowledge with Doctor Torty, swearing him to
secrecy. Having borne the noble name of de Savigny, she does not
want that name sullied by scandal, reason enough to call upon the
doctor's discretion. Even in her dying moments, however, she
recognizes the implications of the situation for other noblemen. In
the past, the adulterous servant would simply have been cast into a
dungeon, forgotten, and there the matter would have ended: "But
at present, we are no longer masters of our own domain. We no
longer have our expeditious, silent justice, and in no way do I want

the scandal and publicity of your own justice, Doctor. I prefer to leave them in one another's arms, happy and free of me, I prefer to die enraged than to think, as I die, that the local nobility would face the ignominy of having a poisoner in its ranks" (p. 119). The dying noblewoman proves stronger than the jealous wife.

Barbey's lifelong preoccupation with exceptional cases has been shown repeatedly in the discussion of his various novels. In "Le bonheur dans le crime," Barbey deviates from his generally pessimistic view of life to present an example of happiness which can only be described as exceptional. The happiness achieved by Savigny and Hauteclaire is authentic to the point of standing up under the scrutiny of Doctor Torty and of confounding the cynical doctor, leaving him at a total loss to explain this unique experience. Obsessed with absolutes, most often of a tragic nature, Barbey shows here an absolute happiness which at the same time is an absolute evil, since it is based on a criminal act. He does not overtly condone this act, but one senses that he would condemn the Comte de Savigny less for his illicit relationship with Hauteclaire than for violating the rules of class loyalty and thus abetting the deterioration of the nobility. One also senses his fascination with two individuals who have the intelligence and the "good" fortune to commit evil with impunity. Despite their transgressions, and perhaps because of them, Barbey regards these individuals as superior, privileged beings. Confronted with the crumbling of the old nobility, Barbey seems to be suggesting the slow emergence of a new nobility, made up of women such as Vellini (in *Une vieille maîtresse*), Calixte Sombreval (in *Un prêtre marié*) and Hauteclaire Stassin. The mystical type of nobility represented by Calixte is paralleled by the nobility of passion embodied by Vellini and Hauteclaire. "Le bonheur dans le crime," perhaps the most credible and powerful of the *Diaboliques*, also contains an essentially pessimistic statement about life. Barbey seems to be saying here that happiness — defined as total compatibility with a member of the opposite sex — can be attained only by truly exceptional beings ruthless enough to destroy other human beings obstructing their pursuit of happiness.

V *"Le dessous de cartes d'une partie de whist"*

The events of this story ("The Underside of the Cards at a Game

of Whist'') are narrated in an exclusive Paris salon which contrasts rather strikingly with those events. As frequently occurs, considerable space is given to a description of the milieu where the
action took place, namely Valognes. Because the only semblance of
passion in this town is a craze for whist, the prolonged stay of
Marmor de Karkoël, a grand master of whist, is most welcome. The
game is played from morning until night at the homes of various
members of the nobility. On the surface, it would seem that nothing
could have brought together Karkoël and the Comtesse de Stasseville, who are coolly polite toward one another. Therefore what follows seems to be a listing of bizarre effects without any definitive
indication of causes. It is strongly implied however, that the causes
have much to do with a clandestine relationship between Karkoël
and the Comtesse.

A game of whist is interrupted by someone who notices the
remarkable brilliance of the Comtesse's diamond and the narrator
suddenly recalls having seen Marmor pouring poison into a ring
some two weeks earlier. In the background, one hears the caver-
nous cough of the Comtesse's teenage daughter, Herminie, who is
gravely ill, while the Comtesse chews quietly on reseda stems.
Shortly afterward, Herminie dies from a chest disease, as does the
Comtesse; and Marmor leaves for India in the service of his government. The disappearance of the principals leaves the way open for
the most horrendous conjectures about precisely what took place
between them. It is known, however, that the Comtesse had begun
hating her daughter; but the reasons for this hatred are never ascertained. After the Comtesse's death, an infant's body is found in the
very flower-stand which contained the resedas she would chew
whenever she played whist. Such are the essentials of what is revealed by the narrator, the story concluding with a few remarks
made by his horrified listeners.

"Le dessous de cartes..." contains one of Barbey's most eloquent tributes to Valognes, the Norman town where he spent part
of his youth and to which he returned frequently in later years. At
one time, Valognes was "the most profoundly and ferociously
aristocratic town in France" (p. 134). The words are spoken by the
narrator to a group of noblemen and noblewomen assembled in a
chic Parisian salon and the reader easily detects a note of one-
upmanship in his homage to a small provincial town: "Never have I
seen anything quite like it. Neither our Faubourg Saint-Germain,

nor the Place Bellecour in Lyon, nor the three or four large cities commended for their exclusive and lofty aristocratic spirit could give you any idea of this little town of six thousand souls which, before 1789, had fifty emblazoned carriages proudly circulating in its streets" (*Ibid.*). It would not be presumptuous to state that the narrator here is Barbey's spokesman, since the views of both are identical: one has only to compare Barbey's critical works with the ideas expressed here to recognize the identity. No effort is made to conceal the narrator's partisanship, since he refers to the prejudices of the nobility as "sublime social truths" (*Ibid.*) including the prejudice against those who are not noblemen and the *a priori* decision not to marry beneath one's social class. Barbey admires the seeming gratuitousness of this total dedication to an ideal, the apparent useless sacrifice of young ladies who prefer to die as spinsters than to tarnish their coats of arms through misalliances. This lofty isolation from the rest of society is the logical, albeit extreme, consequence of the aristocracy's belief in the aristocratic idea.

Except for prolonged sojourns by members of the English nobility, drawn to Valognes by its tranquility, its rigid propriety and its aloofness, nothing broke the terrible monotony of the little town whose sole activity was card-playing, "the last passion of worn-out souls" (p. 138). It is therefore a highly inappropriate milieu for passions and adventures, but the dichotomy between the fastidious propriety of Valognes and the horrors it conceals is the very basis of the story. Karkoël's mania for whist and his superiority as a player transform him rapidly from unknown foreigner to local celebrity. No one in his circle of acquaintances is concerned about his past or about the real Karkoël. Approximately twenty-eight years old, he was born in the foggy mountains of the Shetland Isles, the scene of Walter Scott's "sublime story," "The Pirate" (p. 150). Thus, even the scanty details known about him underscore the mysterious nature of a man who remained persistently undecipherable to the "Valognais," among whom he spent four years. His entire existence centered upon whist-playing to the apparent exclusion of all other activities, and at his table the game was raised to the level of an art form. Curiously enough, only one woman never invited him to her country home and rarely to her town house — the Comtesse de Stasseville.

With eyes the color of emerald, a sharp wit, a reputation beyond reproach, and an ability to remain unruffled by anything at all, the

Comtesse is the very type of the female dandy. Hers is a "stagnant nature" (p. 148), soberly fulfilling her external religious and social duties, secretive, aloof: "Nothing from within threw any light on the woman's bearing. Nothing external had any repercussions within" (p. 149). After setting forth the Comtesse's basic characteristics, the narrator develops a series of conjectures which might apply to other female characters in Barbey, including Vellini (*Une vieille maîtresse*), Alberte ("Le rideau cramoisi"), the Duchesse de Sierra-Leone ("La vengeance d'une femme") among others. According to the narrator, the Comtesse prefers to seek out the bottom, rather than the surface of things; she is "one of those beings destined to occult cohabitations, plunging into life as great swimmers dive and swim underwater" (pp. 154–55).

Proceeding from the particular to the general, the narrator goes on to make an impassioned plea in defense of those who deliberately choose to wear a mask, arguing that perhaps individuals such as the Comtesse enjoy lying for its own sake, just as others like art for art's sake: "I am convinced that for certain souls, there is the happiness of imposture. There is a frightful but intoxicating bliss in the idea of lying and deceiving, in the thought that they alone *know their true selves* and that society is duped by the games they play, the expenses of which are offset by all the pleasures of contempt" (p. 155). These ideas can be looked upon as a major departure from the obsessive quest for communion or communication so frantically sought after by most of Barbey's characters. These ideas can also be seen, perhaps more accurately, as the height of individualism, a form of self-sufficiency and a manifestation of intense scorn for society, even for a society of noblemen. Barbey himself, it should be recalled, stood in lofty isolation from his age.

The views expressed by the narrator are confirmed when he returns to Valognes a few years after the events. The Chevalier de Tharsis, who had known the Comtesse de Stasseville and Marmor de Karkoël, summarizes the conjectures and rumors. It appears that she was indeed his mistress, states the Chevalier, adding: "The Comtesse was a first-rate hypocrite. She was a hypocrite just as a woman is a blonde or a brunette, she was a born hypocrite" (p. 166). This categorical statement is the only certainty in the minds of those who were in daily contact with the Comtesse and Karkoël and who were taken in by the sinister games played by a couple whose disdain for society reminds us of Savigny and Hauteclaire in "Le bonheur dans le crime." The important questions remain unanswered: did Karkoël love the Comtesse? Did he love Herminie? Or did he love both? Where did the infant come from, whose body was found after the Comtesse's death? If the infant had been killed, who was the murderer?

Initially, a reader may well be perplexed by "Le dessous de cartes d'une partie de whist" or he may fear having been duped by the narrator; the story may also give a sense of incompleteness. It is my own conviction that the best defense of the underlying esthetic has been offered by Barbey himself: "What emerges from these hidden, muffled dramas ... is more lurid and takes a stronger hold on one's imagination and memory than if the entire drama had been played out under your eyes. What you don't know centuples the impression of what you do know. Unless I am mistaken, hell seen through an air-vent must be much more ghastly than if you could take in the whole of it with one all-encompassing look" (pp. 132–133). A glimpse of hell through an air-vent would be a fitting description of Barbey's entire fictional world.

VI   *"A un dîner d'athées"*

The story is divided into two parts of equal interest. The ex-soldier Mesnilgrand, friendly with a notorious group of atheists, is seen entering a church and giving an unnamed object to a priest. On the following Friday, the atheists gather at the home of Mesnilgrand for their weekly dinner. These reunions are infamous throughout the region for the sacrilegious and scabrous stories exchanged by extremely bitter men, whose hopes and careers have been broken by the fall of the Empire in 1814. Although he has been in general agreement with these acquaintances, Mesnilgrand differs from them mostly by his fairness in religious matters. When asked to explain his recent presence in a church, he relates a series of events which began during the war with Spain in 1808. Major Ydow, serving in the same regiment as Mesnilgrand, was accompanied in his campaigns by his mistress, an exceptionally attractive woman called La Rosalba and nicknamed "La Pudica." When the woman became the sexual focal point of the regiment, Ydow remained impassive, either unknowing or guarding his jealousy.

When La Rosalba became pregnant, there was considerable

uncertainty about the child's real father, since the lady had be-
friended virtually every officer in the regiment. Upon the death of
the child, Ydow was grief-stricken, convinced that the child was
his. Shortly afterward, Mesnilgrand visited La Rosalba one evening
as she was sealing a letter intended for her current lover. At the
sound of Ydow's footsteps, Mesnilgrand vanished into a closet.
After reading the letter, Ydow became possessed by irrational rage.
During the ensuing struggle, La Rosalba stirred up his rage still further by shouting that she never loved him and that the child was not
his, but that of Mesnilgrand. Ydow's fury atained the level of
paroxysm; he crushed beneath his boot the crystal urn containing
the embalmed heart of the deceased child. Other atrocities followed, including the "sealing" of La Rosalba with the wax she had
used to seal her letter — Ydow's idea of poetic justice, since he
sealed her precisely where she had sinned. Mesnilgrand bolted from
the closet, killed Ydow, and rushed out to join the troops responding to a surprise attack. Before leaving, he instructed the maid to
summon the surgeon, picked up the child's heart, and took it with
him to keep for several years. This was the object he was seen
giving to a priest, with the request that it be buried in sacred
ground. There is none of the anticipated sarcasm from his listeners
who are left pensive by his narrative.

One of the most engaging characters in "A un dîner d'athées" is
the forty-year-old Mesnilgrand, whose hopes for a brilliant career
crumbled with the Empire. So promising was his future, so furious-
ly did he pursue his career goals, that those who knew him expected
either suicide or insanity would result; but he shocked everyone by
plunging into art work with characteristic fury. Despite the vagaries
of fate, his esence remained unchanged:

He was profoundly aristocratic. He was not only an aristocrat by birth, by
caste, by social rank; he was an aristocrat *by nature,* as he was *himself* and
not someone else, as he would have been, if he were the lowliest shoemaker
in town. Lastly, he was an aristocrat, as Heinrich Heine says, "by his
grand manner of feeling" and not in a bourgeois way, like the newly rich
who thrive on external distinctions. (p. 182)

Mesnilgrand's instinctive, all-pervasive, thoroughgoing aristocracy
went beyond titles. The nobility of Valognes long remembered the
posh reception at which he had himself announced as "Monsieur le

Duc de Mesnilgrand," on the pretext that since titles were in vogue, he had selected the one which suited his fancy. The point was made, and the petty vanity diminished, at least for a time.

Like Brassard in "Le rideau cramoisi," Mesnilgrand has considerably more depth than one would have thought. During the dinner described at some length in the first half of the story, the Abbé Reniant, an apostate, recounts that he once threw some consecrated hosts to swine as a deliberate sacrilege. Mesnilgrand corrects him, arguing that the act was meaningless rather than sacrilegious, because Reniant did not believe the hosts to be sacred. We also find Mesnilgrand admiring the actions of Joséphine Tesson who, during the Revolution, concealed hosts on her person, so that priests could have access to them at will. Others are titillated at the thought of a plump young virgin carrying a box of hosts in her bosom, while Mesnilgrand is impressed by the sincerity and depth of the girl's convictions. By this sense of fairness, he contrasts sharply with his acquaintances and acquires increasing credibility, a quality essential to any narrator, especially in the case of one required to relate the horrors of Major Ydow and La Rosalba.

The weekly dinners which have earned a certain notoriety are given by the old reprobate, Mesnilgrand *père,* as feasts for his son the ex-soldier. These meals, held every Friday, deliberately combine sumptuous dishes of meat and fish so that the Church's laws of abstinence may be blatantly transgressed. There is an important element of social history in this description, since Barbey has captured for us the feelings of men overpowered by historical forces. With the disappearance of the Empire and the Revolution crushed by reactionaries, these men lost their positions, their hopes, their foothold in society. Powerless, defeated, humiliated, they returned to Valognes as frustrated embittered souls; of varying political persuasions, they were in profound agreement only in their atheism, the "absolute and furious" atheism of the early nineteenth century (p. 189). In the Middle Ages, they would have become mercenaries or soldiers of fortune, but in the age in which they lived, they were compelled to champ at the bit and to repress their superhuman rage. This feeling was shared by Mesnilgrand *père,* for since his son "had remained caught like a Titan under the overturned mountain of the Empire, he had toward him the respect of a man who has weighed life in all the precision-scales of scorn and who found that nothing is more beautiful, after all, than human strength crushed by the stupidity of fate!'' (pp. 187–88). It is for this son that Mesnilgrand *père* brings together approximately twenty-five table companions every Friday — defrocked priests, doctors of the materialist school, a "people's representative" who had voted for the death of the King, "a Sanhedrin of devils" (p. 192). Such are the people whom the younger Mesnilgrand has seemingly deceived by his unwonted appearance in the church at Valognes and it is this apparent deception which he succeeds in justifying by relating the story of La Rosalba.

The very name "La Rosalba," with its intimations of innocence, purity and chastity, is the first term of the dichotomy between appearance and reality which is one of the bases for so many of Barbey's stories. The irony resulting from this gap is heightened by the woman's nickname, "la Pudica" ("the Modest One"). The nickname is neither gratuitous nor cynical, since modesty (*pudeur*) is indeed her outstanding characteristic, permeating her considerable sexuality, becoming an integral part of the pleasures she gives and receives. She is forever repeating how terribly ashamed she feels, while performing the boldest sexual acts: "She would have come out of an orgy of bacchantes, just like Innocence from its first sin. Even in the vanquished woman, lying half-dead in a swoon, one saw the embarrassed virgin, with the ever-fresh grace of her agitation and the dream-like charm of her blush . . ." (p. 212). This curious mixture of modesty and voluptuousness had been for Mesnilgrand a source of intense excitement. Like other diabolical women, she embodies absolute evil, but her modesty gives her a touch of Heaven not found in others, for she is "the wildest of courtesans, with the face of one of Raphael's most celestial madonnas" (p. 213).

Major Ydow is among the most sinister of the mysterious male figures in all of Barbey's work, capable of worse atrocities even than Sombreval in *Un prêtre marié* or Père Riculf in *Une histoire sans nom*. Barbey notes his resemblance to a certain bust of Antinoüs in which the sculptor had capriciously encrusted emeralds in the place of the eyes. Extremely handsome, lucky in gambling, lucky with women, Ydow has the haughtiness of a conqueror, as well as a profoundly untrustworthy look in his green, tiger-like eyes — in short, a number of personal traits inspiring antipathy among his fellow-officers. Impassive in the face of Rosalba's daily betrayals, he shows no trace whatever of jealousy until he is overcome by a volcanic rage and perpetrates one of the most cruel acts of revenge one can imagine by sealing Rosalba's sexual organs with boiling wax. The description of the scene barely takes up one paragraph and is followed by an equally brief account of Mesnilgrand's response, which is to kill Ydow on the spot. Any lengthy discussion of Ydow's act is risky, since so little is known about his inner life. Barbey has made no attempt to outline the tortuous path which led the man to commit such an intensely repulsive act and ultimately the best commentary on the incident may well be that provided by Félicien Rops in the illustrations accompanying certain editions of the *Diaboliques*.

Despite its obvious preoccupation with erotic horror, "A un dîner d'athées" can be interpreted as a profoundly religious work, for it exemplifies something approximating the ultimate in evil. It depicts evil on a purely spiritual plane as a deliberate rejection of God, compounded by "blasphemy," i.e., willful insults addressed to a God in whom the atheists have ceased believing. On a human level, evil is portrayed in one of its extreme forms as the wanton destruction of an individual. When Mesnilgrand completes his narrative, a hush falls over the group of listeners, no sarcasm is forthcoming, and Barbey poses a rhetorical question: "Did these atheists finally understand that even if the Church had been established only to receive the hearts — dead or alive — with which one does not know what to do, that in itself would justify its existence?" (p. 228).

VII   *"La Vengeance d'une femme"*

During the late eighteen-forties, a young Parisian beau, Robert de Tressignies, follows a prostitute to a hovel. From the moment he sees her, Tressignies, the experienced observer, suspects that there is something unusual about this woman. His suspicion becomes a conviction when he recognizes that her beauty is truly out of the ordinary and when her sexual performance is carried out with a sense of purpose far exceeding considerations of monetary gain. He quickly learns that she is the Duchesse de Sierra-Leone, the very woman he was able to glimpse from a distance three years earlier when they both were spending the season at Saint-Jean-de-Luz. She relates to him the dreadful sequence of events which has led to her present social status. Married to one of the greatest Spanish

grandees, a man she did not love in the least, she soon found herself
involved in a deep and intense platonic relationship with Don Esteban, Marquis of Vasconcellos. The Duke, beside himself with
wounded pride, killed Don Esteban and had his heart devoured by
dogs in the presence of the Duchess. Crushed by the base, monstrous nature of the Duke's action, the Duchess vowed that her life
would be a permanent vengeance. After considering all the means
at her disposal, she selected the one which would inflict the greatest
pain on her husband's enormous pride and boundless sense of
honor: she became a street-walker in Paris. She reveals her identity
to all who visit her and has resolved that she will die a prostitute
and that her vengeance will be assured and complete. Within
months, she dies a horrible death from a disease she has contracted
while satisfying her thirst for vengeance. At her request, her tomb
bears the words "repentant prostitute" in addition to her full
name.

"La vengeance d'une femme" is yet another challenge to the
prudishness of nineteenth-century literature. The narrative is preceded by a few prefatory pages in which Barbey laments the lack of
boldness of contemporary writers. Literature does not even express
one half of the crimes committed every single day, writers are inti-
midated by subjects such as incest (a daily occurrence according to
Barbey, in every social class), and novelists lack the courage to
write stories dealing with the modern-day counterparts of Oedipus
or Agrippina. If only writers "dared to dare," the novel would
have its own Tacitus, its own Suetonius. Furthermore, crime has
lost its horrifying poetry because of what is called social progress;
hence it becomes most difficult for the writer to restore to crime the
tragic poetry it once had: "However, the crimes of extreme civilization are assuredly more atrocious than those of extreme barbarous-
ness, by virtue of their refinement, the corruption they suppose and
their superior degree of intellectualism" (p. 231). This type of
crime addresses itself much more to the intellect than to the senses,
hence to that which is most profound in us. The novelist who is dar-
ing enough can draw a new kind of tragic effect ("tout un genre de
tragique inconnu") from these crimes and "La vengeance d'une
femme" offers an example of a bloodless, civilized crime while
illustrating, precisely, this "tragique inconnu" (p. 231).

Barbey exploits to the fullest the preposterous gap between
appearance and reality in the person of the Duchess turned prosti-

tute. She has indeed the figure of the latter, but her face is "capable of arresting desire with its haughtiness and of petrifying into respect the most ardent lust" (p. 237). This general statement is substantiated when Tressignies — the roué, the cynic, the dandy — discovers the true identity of the woman whose sexual favors he has just bought: "By revealing herself, the Duchess had swept away the courtesan! To him, there was nothing left but the Duchess — but in what a state! Soiled, destroyed, lost, adrift at sea, a woman who had fallen from a greater height than the Leucatas Cliff into a sea of filth, a hopelessly foul and disgusting woman" (p. 244). The man who, just a few moments earlier, had received the most intense carnal pleasure from this woman is now "petrified into respect." He remembers most vividly the inaccessible socialite of three summers ago at Saint-Jean-de-Luz. Tressignies has become literally incapable of setting a finger upon the erstwhile harlot. This metamorphosis of a rake into a stunned observer goes beyond Barbey's passion for recording the effects of the past upon the present; it is a statement about the essence of nobility.

Barbey's obsession with noble blood has too often been dismissed as irrelevant or anachronistic. Tressignies' reaction is yet another reminder (there are many such reminders in these novels and stories) that for Barbey, nobility has a power, an authenticity and a reality not contingent upon the existence of a monarchy. It is a reality transcending accidents of time or place, a reality so unquestionable that a prostitute who reveals her identity as a noblewoman becomes sacred, untouchable. Tressignies is thunderstruck by the revelation, and merely to touch the woman he now knows to be the Duchess of Sierra-Leone would be an unthinkable transgression.

In order to worsen the degradation which the Duchess has deliberately wrought, Barbey pulls out all the stops, giving her and the Duke an imposing though fanciful genealogy. The Duke's lineage antedates that of the most illustrious dynasties which have ruled over Spain — Castile, Aragon, Transtamare, Austria and Bourbon. He is a descendant of the old Gothic kings and is related, through Brunhilde, to the Merovingians of France. His blood is that unadulterated *sangre azul,* now virtually extinct. The Duchess is the last of her line, as is typical and significant with so many of Barbey's characters. She is by birth a Turre-Cremata, a relative of the Grand Inquisitor Torquemada who, in her own words, "inflicted fewer tortures, during his entire life, than there are in this accursed breast" (p. 246). These details may appear superfluous, yet they are essential to a full appreciation of the story's meaning. For Barbey, there exists a well-defined hierarchy in society, just as in matters of morality there are varying degrees of good and evil. The moral and the social spheres are inseparable, since a person's social status affects the morality of his or her actions. Being a member of the nobility entails obligations as well as privileges, and one of those obligations is of course to set an example for others to emulate. Since both the Duke and the Duchess have an illustrious lineage, their commitment to the proper values (as defined by the Catholic Church) must be unswerving. It therefore follows that the Duke's murder of Don Esteban is a most heinous crime and that the reaction of the Duchess, while meting out a retribution which is far from totally unwarranted, constitutes a precipitous drop from a social and moral pinnacle.

Before the appearance of Don Esteban, the marital life of the Duke and Duchess was exemplary, though for the Duchess, quite dull. The marriage had been arranged by their two families, and feeling played no part whatever in this alliance. The discovery of love with Don Esteban reveals to the Duchess a realm of feeling which she has never experienced. Their mutual love is quite out of the oridnary, for it is at once "burning and chaste," chivalrous, almost mystical, as the Duchess recalls:

It is true that we were both barely twenty years old and that we were from the country of Bivar, Ignatius of Loyola and Saint Theresa. Ignatius, the Knight of the Virgin, did not love the Queen of Heaven more purely than Vasconcellos loved me; and, for my part, I felt for him something of the ecstatic love which Saint Theresa had for her Divine Spouse. Adultery? Nonsense! The thought never once crossed our minds. Our hearts beat so high in our breasts, we lived in an atmosphere of feelings so transcendental and so lofty, that we experienced none of the evil desires and sensuality of commonplace relationships. (p. 249)

Her sense of marital duty compels the Duchess to urge her husband to prohibit Don Esteban from visiting the household, since he has begun to love her in a manner she terms "insolent." The Duke's response ("He would not dare!" p. 248), scornful of destiny and of Don Esteban both, precipitates her decision to implore Esteban to "dare." Thus, they pursue their relationship until the Duke, in a fit of jealous rage, has two of his slaves kill his rival in a most brutal and hideous fashion. The Duchess does not hesitate at all: the Duke must be crucified in his pride, his name must be dishonored, cruel vengeance will be her life's work. Even the modern reader will be struck by the scope and intensity of the Duchess' vengeance which is for her an all-consuming force, a passion to which she gives herself with complete singleness of purpose and with total lucidity. It is an extreme, an absolute, the most any woman could do in the way of vengeance; and the reactions of Tressignies might well be those of the author: "He was frightened by this horrible sublimity ["ce sublime horrible"], for intensity of feeling pushed to this point is sublime. But it is the sublimity of hell" (p. 254).

VIII   Les Diaboliques: *Conclusion*

Les Diaboliques contains the quintessence of Barbey's genius as a storyteller, for the work exemplifies his ability to bring about shock effects with rare skill. He also excels here at the tale told within a tale, recording the interaction between narrator and listener and the interplay between past and present. Perhaps more important, the work signals Barbey's evolution away from a reliance on the *fantastique* to evoke the effects of Satan's presence in the world. Satanism is cast in purely human terms by means of characters who signify absolute evil. These characters are not "bewitched" or "possessed" as were some of their predecessors in previous stories; they are single-mindedly obsessed by a given passion, the consequences of which they are destined to play out to a logical extreme. The equation of passion with satanism could hardly be clearer, yet occult forces do not intervene in human affairs; the pomps and works of Satan originate in the human soul. The meaning is clear: in the human heart reside potentialities which can best be described as "diabolical" and which find full expression in paroxysms of passion.

In *Les Diaboliques,* there is a spirit of revolt against the spiritual order of things, a spirit of concupiscence, the very spirit of evil itself, as well as an atmosphere of mystery and sensuality, a combination of elements best synthesized by Barbey d'Aurevilly and Baudelaire. *Les Diaboliques* also points up the gap between the superhuman characters of Barbey's fictional universe and what was, for him, the insufferable banality of the contemporary world. Condemn as he might the evil committed by his diabolical men and women, *they* at least had the requisite boldness to live out their passions to the fullest. Monomaniacs, absolutists of passion, there is nothing mediocre about them. That in itself was enough to recommend them to Barbey's everlasting fascination ... and to ours.

IX   Une histoire sans nom

Une histoire sans nom (A Story Without a Name) appeared in 1882 and was well received by the reading public. The reviews were mixed, though most critics acknowledged Barbey's talent. The most insightful article was doubtless the one written by Henry Trianon for *Le Constitutionnel* of October 29, 1882, where he states in part: "... one wonders from what well of darkness, from what action or from what thought this somber reflection might come, which casts black crepe on the works of Monsieur Barbey d'Aurevilly.... Catholicism may have supporters who are more authoritative than he; but it does not have any who are more energetic or more determined. And yet there is suffering in his attitude, and a kind of muffled revolt." These remarks could be applied to many of Barbey's works, but they seem particularly fitting as a commentary on *Une histoire sans nom*.

During the seventeen-eighties, a Capuchin monk, Père Riculf, disappears from the tiny hamlet where he has been preaching a Lenten retreat. His host family, the widowed Madame de Ferjol and her sixteen-year old daughter Lasthénie are mystified by his abrupt departure, then forget about the strange priest who had remained aloof throughout his entire stay with them. A short time later, Lasthénie begins suffering from a mysterious illness; it is discovered that she is pregnant under circumstances she is unable to explain to her horrified mother. Madame de Ferjol denies her daughter any compassion whatever and refuses to forgive her for what she regards as a most heinous sin. Isolated from any meaningful human contact, Lasthénie gives birth to a stillborn child, descends slowly into idiocy, and commits suicide. Twenty-five years later, Mme de Ferjol learns that the late Père Riculf had raped Lasthénie while she was sleepwalking, had become an outlaw, then had expiated his sins in a Trappist monastery. Possessed by hate for the man who caused Lasthénie's dishonor and death, she profanes his grave and dies without repenting of her hatred.

It is unwise to discuss *Une histoire sans nom* without making clear at the outset that the story's sensationalism is quite secondary and that the work succeeds as a study of total human isolation with its inevitably tragic consequences. The setting intensifies this horrible solitude, for the events take place in a lonely hamlet located in a tiny valley surrounded by the Cévennes mountains of central France:

Like all scenes which have something fantastic about them at night, this one had its own fantastic aura. These circular mountains, with summits so close they almost kissed one another, could have upon the imagination the effect of a circle of Giant Fairies, standing up, whispering in one another's ears, like women standing up after a visit, about to embrace as they exchange their parting words. The scene had this effect particularly since the mist rising from the streams irrigating the grass placed a white burnous of pearly fog on the vast green dresses of these Giant Fairies, streaked with the silver of the streams. (p. 298)

The melancholy nature of this scene is what should be remembered, rather than its poetry, for Barbey will insist repeatedly on the oppressive effect of the mountains on the village lying engulfed at their base as though at the bottom of a giant funnel. So high are the obtrusive mountains that sunlight barely filters into this lost village, where there is, on occasion, still darkness at noon.

Madame de Ferjol, Lasthénie, and their servant Agathe are the sole inhabitants of an enormous gray house — empty, cold, lonely, with the mountainside directly behind its tiny garden. Mme de Ferjol and Lasthénie seldom leave the house and no visitors have enlivened it since the death of Monsieur de Ferjol several years earlier. "Going out" means a walk in the mountains or, more frequently, attending church services. In this setting, Père Riculf, inscrutable, formidable, eloquent, gives thunderous sermons on the grimmest truths of the Catholic faith, reminding his listeners that hell and damnation are real, relentlessly holding forth, day after lengthy Lenten day, on the awesome powers of the Prince of Darkness. Riculf preaches in the eerie atmosphere of a dimly lit thirteenth-century church, where the statues, draped in white for the Lenten season, contribute much to the general ghostliness.

Riculf himself remains a shadowy figure throughout the novel, always seen from the vantage point of the other characters or of the omniscient narrator who never allows us a glimpse of the man's

inner reality. He has the same haughty pride, the same imperial de-
meanor as the Abbé de la Croix-Jugan in *L'Ensorcelée,* extending
his hand with lordly authority, seeming to *demand* alms rather than
requesting them humbly, as preaching monks usually do. Born to
command, he seems capable of anything. One is curious about his
motivations for becoming a priest, for there is nothing priestly
about his overbearing personality. Even his hosts feel ill at ease in
his presence. One regrets that the character is not fleshed out, since
he is so awesome, strong-willed, and prone to absolutes. After his
disappearance from the home of Mme de Ferjol, he leaves the
Capuchin Order to lead a life of dissipation and banditry, after
which he seeks the most extreme means of expiating his sins by
entering a Trappist monastery and observing its highly rigorous
Rule.

We become somewhat better acquainted with Riculf's victim, the
frail young Lasthénie de Ferjol, emotionally atrophied because the
mother whom she loves but fears will not tolerate any expression of
feeling. Lasthénie seeks in piety and prayer the solace, strength,
and warmth denied her by a mother obsessed by guilt; but she is too
weak to find in prayer the serenity which others, less frail or less
tender, are capable of deriving from an intense religious life.
Devastated by the inexplicable nature of her pregnancy and by her
mother's cruel coldness, she begins a slow descent toward a state of
idiocy. She is comparable to Calixte Sombreval in *Un prêtre marié,*
inasmuch as she too is victimized by a horrendously unjust fate,
overwhelmed by forces she can neither fathom nor control until,
isolated in silent stupor, she slowly commits suicide by planting
needles into her own chest.

The novel is dominated by the unyielding, rigid, despotic figure
of Mme de Ferjol, haunted by the memory of her deceased husband, a man she had loved with a passion which now appears to her
to have been sinful. Fifteen years after her husband's death, her
passion for him has survived; but she conceals and represses this
love with her iron will, striving endlessly to rechannel the passion
into an extremely harsh form of piety. She loves her daughter
fiercely but exercises constant restraint, refusing to express her
love, in part because it never occurs to her that maternal love might
well be integrated into her overall plan of atonement and salvation.
She recognizes too that she loves her daughter more because she is
her husband's child than because she is her own, hence her love for

her daughter, associated in her mind with her "guilty," excessive passion for her husband, would be an added source of guilt if she allowed it to find expression. So all-consuming is the depth of these feelings that it is difficult to convey them persuasively, for the words "obsession" and "compulsion" barely begin to do them justice. Mme de Ferjol has fallen prey to an extreme form of Jansenism, believing to the utmost that whatever merit she might have in the eyes of God depends upon her ability to restrain her feelings, especially the abundance of love she has for her child. She remains unaware that her refusal to show affection toward her daughter causes Lasthénie to feel rejected. Her distorted sense of religious duty allows her to forgive nothing and ceaselessly demands self-mortification.

The gap between the two becomes an abyss when Lasthénie's pregnancy is discovered. Silence gives way to hysteria, as Mme de Ferjol begins shouting to her daughter that she has dishonored herself, that she is lost and damned, beseeching her, however, to reveal the identity of her "lover." The mother is transformed into a living horror, since Lasthénie can neither reveal the name of her seducer nor alter her condition. Mme de Ferjol is petrified into a state of permanent, exacerbated anger. A compelling explanation for this anger is proffered by the narrator when he tells us that Mme de Ferjol had become pregnant before marrying. She therefore sees her daughter's pregnancy as a punishment for her own sin, and one understands why she feels as "dishonored" by Lasthénie's pregnancy as does the girl; it is an obvious case of over-identification, deftly handled by a skilled novelist.

In Mme de Ferjol's ongoing self-interrogation regarding the identity of the seducer, she begins to suspect Riculf, strives vainly to keep the thought out of her mind, until it becomes obsessive, hallucinatory. Dishonor, unacceptable in itself, would become infamy and sacrilege if it were indeed true that Lasthénie had had sexual relations with a priest. Tortured by persistent thoughts of this possibility, but aware of the need to avoid scandal, she decides that a return to her old Château of Olonde in Normandy is imperative; after the move to Normandy, she is still a monomaniac, hell-bent on maintaining complete secrecy about what she views as an unspeakable horror. Even Agathe, her devoted servant, will know nothing about the imminent birth of the illegitimate child. The Château d'Olonde provides a prison-like, total solitude, with the mother acting as the daughter's gaoler; the house acquires a tomb-like silence, becoming itself a tomb, a veritable house of the dead. When Lasthénie does give birth to the stillborn child, Mme de Ferjol holds it up for her daughter to behold, and shouts at her with cruel pride: "Here is your crime and its atonement!" (p. 335). Small wonder that the girl takes her own life.

The madness does not end here, however, since the epilogue, which takes place a full quarter of a century after these events, offers still more horror. Mme de Ferjol "was a ruin now, but a ruin like the Colosseum. She had its *grandeur* and its majesty" (pp. 348–49). By chance, she meets someone who had known Riculf during his years at the monastery, and who relates to her the truth about her daughter's pregnancy and about Riculf's death as a repentant sinner. Overpowered by grief and remorse upon learning that she herself had caused her daughter's death by refusing to believe in her innocence, she is possessed by a frenzied rage toward Riculf and declares: "If he is in Heaven, I want no part of Heaven!" (p. 362). Shortly thereafter, she dies, unforgiving, in what Barbey calls an "impénitence sublime" (p. 364).

The above discussion should legitimate my argument that *Une histoire sans nom* is a novel about cruelty, destruction, and the absolute solitude which the human condition is capable of creating. Worse than the monstrous sexual abuse of Lasthénie by Riculf is Madame de Ferjol's categorical refusal to express her love for her daughter, a refusal motivated by her irrational sense of guilt and her insane fear of eternal damnation. Her entire life is centered upon her compulsive, hopeless, desperate need to atone for her "excessive" passion for her husband. The novelist has once again handled very well the interplay between past and present. Madame de Ferjol's "sin" goes on tormenting her down the years; and when her own daughter becomes guilty of the same "sin" — pregnancy out of wedlock — the past is resurrected and substituted for the present. By punishing Lasthénie, Mme de Ferjol punishes herself; like Calixte Sombreval in *Un prêtre marié,* Lasthénie becomes the innocent victim of someone else's failings. In Barbey's world, the sins of the parents are indeed visited upon the children. *Une histoire sans nom* also denounces the nefarious effects of Jansenism; while the latter may well have been outmoded as a doctrine by the early part of the nineteenth century, it still functioned as a code of ethics, as a way of life for certain people. Yet, while denouncing

Jansenism, Barbey remained fascinated by it, for it made possible the existence of emotional absolutes, i.e. one of Barbey's lifelong preoccupations.

X   Ce qui ne meurt pas

Ce qui ne meurt pas (What Never Dies), was written in the early eighteen-thirties, but Barbey did not find a publisher for it until 1883. It is discussed here because of its publication date and because the minimal changes Barbey made in the final version of the text indicate clearly enough that he did not disavow the novel's contents. Moreover, by its subject matter, it falls well within the scope of the present chapter. Any attempt to determine the genesis of the novel would prove abortive, given the absence of sufficient documents on what will doubtless remain one of the more obscure periods in the author's life — obscure and tempestuous, for during those years he almost lost his *raison d'être,* since the relationship with Louise was ended. Hence, unless new documents are brought to light, we will never know either the precise nature of that relationship or the amount of autobiographical elements contained in *Ce qui ne meurt pas.*

We can state with some certainty, however, that the novel was influenced by George Sand's *Lélia.* In addition to the oratorical tone, the lush style, Barbey also borrowed from George Sand the main theme, the inability to love, attempting to give it broader application. The intentions of the novelist are made clear in a long-unpublished preface, written in 1835, which amounts to an apologia for the psychological and philosophical novel: analysis of thoughts and feelings rather than descriptions of actions and spectacles — that is what the novel needs, he argues. What Godwin did with his analysis of vanity, Barbey will now do with the feeling of pity. There is an over-reaction here, an exacerbated response to the then current modes of French fiction. One also detects a suspicious dichotomy between the novel and the preface. In the latter, the author professes his disdain for passion, alleging that it lacks moral and esthetic *grandeur;* and yet the novel is a lengthy analysis of passion, its birth, development and demise, all of these occurring not once but twice. One can scarcely regret then (quite the contrary in fact) that the preface remained buried in Barbey's personal papers instead of falling into the hands of his enemies.

Ce qui ne meurt pas was originally entitled *Germaine, ou La Pitié*
at the time of writing in the early thirties. Despite numerous attempts, Barbey did not manage to publish the work until 1883 — a
disheartening lesson, no doubt, for young writers. The novel is a
variation on the theme of the triangle, but treated in a rather unexpected manner. Allan de Cynthry, a mere boy, falls passionately in
love with his adoptive mother, Yseult de Scudemor who, worn
down by life and passion, is incapable of loving. Out of pity, but
also out of a desire to destroy the boy's love, Yseult becomes his
mistress; and she ultimately achieves her purpose. Allan then falls
in love with Camille, Yseult's daughter, whom he loves but briefly;
he too becomes worn out and will henceforth remain incapable of
loving, as will Camille, caught up in the same vortex of affective
impotence. The major concession to external action takes the form
of melodrama when Yseult and Camille each give birth to a child
sired by Allan. Camille's subsequent violent outburst, intended as
one of the high points of the story, does not show the novelist at his
best.

One of the more successful aspects of the novel is the setting.
Though the Normandy of *Ce qui ne meurt pas* lacks the intense
color and the mystery of Barbey's "Normandy novels," we find
here a highly effective use of the countryside as a symbol of human
isolation. The novel opens precisely with a description of the setting: an old castle lost in the swampy, marshy area near Sainte-
Mère-Eglise, invisible to its closest neighbors and not even within
hearing distance of the train-whistle. Our attention is drawn, not to
the entrance of the Château des Saules, but to the view from the
other side, the side overlooking the swamps, from which angle it
appears inaccessible, seeming to rise out of a vast bluish pool like a
white water-fairy (p. 383). A world, then, closed in upon itself;
propitious to reverie, indolence, sensual laissez-faire; with no one
for the characters to hide from, in this amphibious retreat, except
of course from one another; a stifling, suffocating world whose
secret dramas only the reader will witness.

The people who inhabit such a world are referred to by the
author as "civilization's *spoiled* children." The French word used
is "gâté," connoting "over-ripe fruit," and is intended to conjure
up visions of a deteriorated, decadent society, a society whose
members are weak and passive, compared to their ancestors the
Vikings, "Kings of the Sea" (p. 381), an aggressive, robust,

conquering lot. With the advance of civilization, Barbey had argued in the preface, the novelist is reduced to a description of nuances of thought and feeling. Accordingly, he has created characters who lend themselves to such close scrutiny.

Initially a mysterious figure, the Countess Yseult de Scudemor emerges at once calm and indifferent, detached from everything, almost as if she had ceased living. This apathy co-exists with a feeling of superiority shown by a "reserve full of nobility" (p. 391) and by a "patrician expression" (p. 392), the superiority of one who has long practiced perfect self-control. Given such a disposition and the fact of her age — twice that of Allan — she can be expected to dominate Allan once the love-affair is set in motion, and this expectation is fulfilled. This type of strong, aggressive woman — the woman who plays a masculine role with a weak lover — will obsess Barbey all his life.

Weak though Allan may be, he does prevail upon Yseult to bare her soul, thereby revealing a woman whom the world does not know. But she accedes to his demand only because she feels that her confession will destroy his love for her, with the result that his love for her grows stronger. The confession includes the revelation of lesbian tendencies (now past) which brought suffering but proved incapable of dissuading her that a woman's goal in life consists solely of seeking happiness in love. She also confesses that after a brief interlude of sensual fury with her husband, love again left her. She then sought bliss in extra-marital sex. Her adulterous actions combine refinement with masochism, since she vehemently but vainly wishes that she might be the object of defloration for her lover and regrets that she has betrayed her lover before she even knew him. This self-laceration, far from being futile, expresses a quest for the absolute. Allan will soon learn from Yseult to seek insatiably for his own unattainable absolute, even in the face of the irreparable. He will come to detest Camille, for example, because he is not her father — that is, because someone has preceded him in the arms of Yseult. But as Yseult proceeds with her autobiographical monologue, interrupted only by Allan's reactions, her personality comes into clearer focus. By her own admission, she soon becomes disillusioned with her lover because he is too carnal, not sufficiently cerebral. Thus Barbey foreshadows an important theme, not only of his future works, but of the late nineteenth century as well.

Disillusioned, she has yet another bitter cup to drink, the cup of humiliation, since it is her lover and not Yseult who will first cease loving, and she compares this to refinements of cruelty in fate, the buffooneries of an executioner cast in the role of God (p. 438). Small wonder, then, that her pessimism is now quite thorough-going, especially since she has reached that tiring stage when it is five o'clock in the afternoon of life (p. 392). Thrice disillusioned by passion, feeling that religion is a crutch, friendship a hybrid and egotistical phenomenon, what has she to live and strive for?

Allan is similarly predisposed to unhappiness. The author refers to his age as that hermaphroditic age between adolescence and youth, a murky no-man's land, without fixed qualities, hence without identity. And yet the author contradicts himself by endowing his character with an intense cerebral life, an imagination sufficient unto itself. Thus, Allan is withdrawn, at once suffering from and delighting in an isolation which he clings to as a form of identity. One must mention too Allan's physiological anomaly: he has the forehead of Lord Byron because, during pregnancy, his mother remained in a state of uninterrupted contemplation of Byron's portrait. Leaving aside the obvious and awkward lack of verisimilitude, we find here a curious admixture of two mentalities: the cult of Byron — that is, a throwback to early Romanticism and in the detail of the physiological anomaly a looking ahead to the interest in physiology so pervasive in later writers, most notably the Naturalists, such as Goncourt and Zola.

Barbey manages to include Camille too in his universe of guilt. In essence, she is guilty of concealing her beauty, which will someday ensnare the hearts of men: "Wouldn't you say that this age without grace is but a first involuntary ruse on the part of those creatures who, later in life are so cunningly and so voluntarily sly?" (p. 386). While most of us, doubtless, look upon youth as an age of possibilities, or at worse an uncertain, neutral age, Barbey oddly enough finds reason to speak ill of it. And that he should find reason for guilt in the hidden beauty of a young girl reveals the depth of his misogyny.

XI *Themes*

But the novel stands or falls by its treatment of love, since love is really its only major theme. Once again, the conception of love evinced in this novel — written, we must remember, in the early eighteen-thirties — makes of the author not merely a forerunner of the "Decadents" (Huysmans, Villiers de l'Isle-Adam, Remy de Gourmont and others) but a true kindred spirit of these *fin-de-siècle* writers. Early in the novel, the reader observes the unmistakably cerebral nature of this love. Obviously, one could hardly expect that Barbey should, in 1835, have developed *all* of the themes related to cerebral love. The importance of the setting, for instance, is mentioned but once, and cursorily at that, when Yseult, Allan, and Camille embark on a journey to Italy. But this detail is Romanticism pure and simple, for the French writers in the early nineteenth century who did not regard Italy as the land of love and of the heart's desire are indeed exceedingly rare. Likewise, the theme of danger is scarcely mentioned in passing; hence one is a long way from Huysmans' character Des Esseintes who, in order to excite himself while making love to his mistress, a ventriloquist, asks her to simulate the cries of an angry, jealous rival outside the bedroom door.

A more fully developed theme related to this conception of cerebral love is that of knowledge, and the role of its progression in the development and, more particularly, in the destruction of love. To pierce the darkness which surrounds the beloved, to probe the innermost recesses of her heart, her mind and her past — these become the obsessive laws governing Allan, because for a person as cerebral as he, knowledge is a form of possession. Yseult, wiser, complies, aware as she is that to answer *all* of Allan's questions is the equivalent of giving herself to him. In her view, to answer much and to give herself as completely as he wants her will eventually bring about an enormous boredom which in turn should toll the knell for Allan's passion. But Allan has far to go before becoming sated, his quest being ultimately a quest for the infinite. Hence the inadequacy of physical possession is made clear, as well as the inadequacy of a possession as complete as it is humanly possible for one person to possess another. Yet these realities do not prevent illusion from remaining alive in Allan, the illusion consisting of equating Yseult with the infinite — albeit only for a time.

One of Barbey's master-strokes in illustrating his conception of love lies in his linking the two themes of the cerebral and the sickly. Allan becomes quite literally love-sick, and the novelist aptly terms this illness a "cerebral fever." There is far more than mere cleverness here, since Allan's illness marks a major turning point in his relations with Yseult. The onset of the fever occurs when Allan agrees to comply with Yseult's request that he leave the Château des Saules; and the request is made because Yseult, who has not yet given herself to him physically, believes that distance will destroy his passion. She then recognizes her responsibility for his illness, allows him to stay, nurses him and, out of pity, abandons herself to him physically.

One could hardly exaggerate the extreme importance of pain, suffering, and related themes in *Ce qui ne meurt pas*. Much of Barbey's fiction reveals the vast number of variations he was capable of conjuring up on these very themes. Allan's love affair with Yseult is a good case in point, for it amounts to a whole complex of feelings, combining masochism, sadism and even a desire to discover in Yseult a need which he might fill. For Allan, love and suffering are inextricably intertwined; and Barbey expresses this in one of his more lyrical utterances: "Oh! love, love is a kiss, a wound, blood which flows and mixes with blood, a night, nights as well as days, a night such as this, and finally, death!" (p. 497). Even when they reach the ineluctable end of the affair, Allan writes to Yseult that suffering in love is good, "for it is the happiness of martyrdom," while the real misfortune in life is the suffering which accompanies the disintegration of love (p. 633).

Suffering, ultimately, is all that Yseult has given Allan and suffering is all that woman, in Barbey's opinion, is capable of giving. When, for example, during his convalescence, Allan takes Yseult into his arms to put her into a saddle and Yseult cries out, "Allan! you are going to hurt yourself!" the author observes wryly: "Such is the misconception common to all women, when you expose yourself to the good fortune of hurting yourself for them, because you love them unto death!" (p. 476). Thus according to Barbey, woman *must* be sadistic; she is a vampire by nature, and if she does not behave accordingly she will be denounced for her lack of logic. And throughout the novel, the author keeps insisting that suffering is far more enthralling than love or beauty.

Suffering and the related theme of poisoning are central preoccupations in this lengthy novel, and the link between passion and poisoning often has an unmistakably Baudelairian tonality: "The flowers of voluptuousness which he was fatally sucking contained a corrosive, mortal poison, like rose-laurel petals" (p. 501). Little wonder, then, that in 1857 Barbey wrote an "Article justificatif" for *The Flowers of Evil,* or that Baudelaire himself became a reader of Barbey.

Although Allan's passion does eventually die, his weakness, his infatuation, and his masochism prevent him from experiencing some of the reactions which one might expect from an adolescent in love with an older woman. The narrator, however, assumes with considerable complacency the role of recording the various signs of Yseult's advancing age: "Hair rendered ashen by the years, upon a neck which has lost the soft pale azure of beautiful veins; eyes whose flame, in slightly dimmed pupils, is concentrated instead of radiating..." (pp. 407-408). Yes, Barbey finds delight in detailing, with cruelty, the ravages of the years wrought upon Yseult — the ashen hair, the dimmed pupils, shoulders likened to yellowed marble (p. 455). One detects in all of this an unmistakable *delectatio morosa,* particularly if one considers Barbey's insistence and his occasional insidiousness in reminding us of the slow, steady erosion of Yseult's person. Whether he writes that the animation of her face made one forget the wrinkles which were beginning to furrow that face (p. 471), or again that one could easily have forgotten that clay had replaced the marble (p. 529), it is obvious that the narrator has *not* "forgotten," no more than he wants his reader to forget.

The link between love and suffering is carried one step further with the alliance of love and death. Here, the novelist exaggerates the imminence of death, "the seed of death which might, of a sudden, blossom tomorrow" (p. 473). Of course, the exaggeration will eventually be justified, at least in part, through the death of passion (first Allan's passion for Yseult, then that which he comes to feel for Camille), and especially through the death of Yseult herself. But before these deaths do occur, the awkward, tireless repetition of the theme detracts from its ability to move us. And yet, the novelist occasionally strikes a new note, when, for instance, he likens Yseult to "the Zahuri of the Spanish legends who, in a cemetery, sees the corpse itself, under the pall of grass and flowers which covers it" (p. 474).

But clearly the master-stroke in the treatment of this strange alliance, indeed, one of the most striking inventions in the novel, is a parable which has yet to receive the notice it rightly deserves. A fool once fell in love with the blade of a sword, a haughty, cruel

mistress, but as slender, lithe and graceful as a girl. The description
of their relationship bears transcribing:

... the homicide responded to his caresses only with blood; blood in exchange for kisses and embraces, blood on hands, chest and lips, until one
day he ran the sword through himself up to the hilt. Oh! while Allan and
ourselves are pressing against our chests women we love to excess, swords
of pain which tear us asunder, why don't we open our chests deep and wide
enough for love and life to escape all at once? (pp. 501-2)

While the second sentence may be faulted for excessive obvious-
ness, one must praise the novelist for the original, bold image he
created to describe that particular passion which is heightened by
the approach of death, that clairvoyance possessed only by such
men as Barbey and Baudelaire, capable of seeing death in love, love
as death.

Charting the course of Allan's life, that lengthy, painful progression from the most frenzied passion to the inability to love, one
recognizes instantly the strange sameness in destinies of Allan and
Yseult. Both are swept onward in the same quest, hurtling forward,
from failure to failure, never ceasing to hope until they are pum-
meled, beaten into the realization that passion destroys itself as it
destroys those who come under its sway. But passion dies slowly,
and while it is dying, the power of illusion dwindles even more
slowly. When Allan ceases loving Yseult, his lucidity does not prevent him from pretending that he still loves her; he strives desperately and vainly to whip up a feeling which he knows exists no
more. Yet, he goes on for a time, speaking to her about love, yearning to love her, craving to become once again her plaything, but
succeeding only in fooling himself less and less as time passes, until
the reality of his situation compels him to admit that a regret over
things past is not the equivalent of a desire.

Pity which, as stated, originally provided the subtitle of this
novel, bears that unmistakable brand of pessimism and misan-
thropy which runs like a streak through the entire fictional world of
Barbey. Initially, pity serves the apparent function of bringing out
the iron will of Yseult. When Allan makes love to Yseult for the
first time, an act which transcends pure carnality, since Allan is
wildly in love with her, an act in which some other woman could
have lost herself completely (in the opinion of the novelist), Yseult

remains completely unmoved, impervious to pleasure, bored, but willfully carrying out the duty which her pity has dictated. Consistently, obsessively, Barbey stresses the negative aspects of pity, whether he is defining it or showing its manifestations, whether the definitions be poetic or literal: "Pity is love without the happiness which love gives. That is why it is not love!" (p. 464). Or, more poetically, "that eternal Pity — a dove speckled with the colors of the sky whence it descends, but which also has a steel beak and the claws of an eagle, for it builds its nest in human hearts only on condition that it will tear them to pieces!" (p. 445). Thus, pity too is vitiated, sterile as a tree which has stopped bearing fruit, one of the forces, the novel implies, which is in the service of a cruel, implacable Destiny.

Bearing in mind what has just been said about the relationship between Allan and Yseult, there would be little justification in attempting as close an analysis of the relationship between Allan and Camille, given its similarities to the former and given its readily identifiable functions: to bring out the more salient traits of the liaison which developed and deteriorated between Allan and Yseult and to precipitate — melodramatically — the ruin of the three characters. Early in the novel, the narrator establishes quite clearly that even compared to Camille, Allan is the weaker of the two, to the extent that the shape of Allan's body, the cut of his hair could have caused him to be mistaken for a girl. And when we read that Camille could have passed for a boy, the transposition of the sexes is complete; and the concept of the androgyne is announced for the first time in Barbey's works.

The same could be said regarding the theme of incest — the very theme of Barbey's last story, *Une page d'histoire*. For greater accuracy, however, it should be stated that in general the relations described by Barbey merely border on the incestuous. Yseult is Allan's adoptive mother, Camille his adoptive sister. To have made them closer relatives would doubtless have been too explicit for the eighteen-thirties; yet the novelist does become quite explicit as evinced by the following remarks made in his own name: "Almost always, we love only someone who is related to us. It is so rare not to lose our hearts to one of life's flowers which blossomed on the same branch as we" (p. 406). Whereas Allan's particular situation as a near-member of the family afforded Barbey the opportunity of developing two incestuous relationships, the incestuous aspect of

Camille's love for Allan is, until near the end of the novel, much more clearly marked. Despite the ambivalent nature of certain remarks made by Allan to Yseult, despite his fairly obvious desire for union with his mother, or with a mother-figure, it is Camille who thrives on being called "sister" by her lover, it is Camille who repeatedly tells Allan how much his "sister" loves him, it is Camille who calls herself his "incestuous sister," wishing she were his *real* sister, and allowing such thoughts to stir up her passion for him.

The treatment of the theme reaches a climax when, at the end of the novel, Allan writes to Yseult that it was she of whom he had so often thought while making love to Camille: "I had so often been unfaithful to her for you, in my memories, that I thought I might rediscover a feeling I once had with you — the horrible happiness of being guilty. But no! my heart and destiny are inflexible. I wanted incest, and neither my heart nor my senses have had the strength to consummate it" (p. 634). Allan therefore sought Yseult in Camille, Yseult the mother-figure. And one finds, in the passage just quoted, a rather unexpected refinement: upon an incestuous relationship is superimposed an adulterous desire, the nature of which is itself, once again, incestuous.

Ce qui ne meurt pas is one of the rare works in Barbey's total writings from which God is absent, God as Barbey conceived Him, *i.e.,* that fearsome Christian God so intolerant of sensuality. Despite this absence, the atmosphere of the novel remains steeped in guilt, that specifically Catholic guilt, a fruit of forbidden love or illicit passion. It is a kind of guilt which would not occur to that healthy pagan, Théophile Gautier, who could write of love and lust without any discernible fear of eternal damnation.

XII *Critical acclaim*

Ce qui ne meurt pas, published in 1883, added little to Barbey's reputation. It did, however, elicit the enthusiasm of two writers of note, but for contradictory reasons. Léon Bloy, one of the most truculent, thundering, vituperative representatives of Catholicism in French literature, hailed the work as eminently Catholic and moral, seeing in it an accurate portrayal of the ravages of passion, and arguing vehemently that Barbey had gone beyond Dante in describing what Dante never saw, namely the "tenth circle of Hell," which consists of prostituting two things, the essence of which is supernatural: pity and love.[2] Oscar Wilde translated the novel, adding a preface in which he wrote: "Barbey had a profound respect for the Devil; and his sober sense of sin adds a relish to the misdemeanors of his characters that can only inspire envy in the breasts of those readers whose pleasures are not so salted. These sins are introduced for their theatrical value rather than their psychological significance..."[3] Already in the eighteen-thirties, Barbey had written a novel which would baffle his readers a half-century later. Léon Bloy and Oscar Wilde: one could hardly imagine a more disparate pair of admirers.

CHAPTER 5

Literary Criticism

I *Introduction*

T HE gap between Barbey's dreams and the reality of everyday life, so obvious in his fiction, is no less evident in his forty-odd volumes of literary criticism. Over the years, the gap became a chasm, his expectations of literature being hardly ever fulfilled by his contemporaries. As might be anticipated, there is much rancor and bitterness in his essays, but they also contain a surprising amount of enthusiasm and praise. For half a century, Barbey was a professional critic, writing for various periodicals; and in most of his articles he goes well beyond the confines of the book-review, consistently relating the book being reviewed to broader issues of a literary, religious, moral, or political nature. This ongoing concern with broader issues, on which he had well-defined and clearly articulated views, is in itself a compelling reason for studying his criticism a century later.[1]

The vagaries of his literary career have been outlined in the first chapter of the present work; but it is necessary to underscore his constant, intense frustration over the limited possibilities which the age of the bourgeoisie offered a man like himself, an aristocrat by temperament. He found journalism onerous but he enjoyed the immediate communication with a literate public and used it as a forum to expound his highly personal opinions. Before 1852, he wrote mostly on political, historical or philosophical works, while the bulk of his later critical writings deals with literary works of the contemporary period. The preface to the first volume of his collected essays, *Les Oeuvres et les Hommes,* published in 1860, sets the tone:

This is criticism which can be mistaken, but which at least will deceive no one. It is criticism without mittens, without felt slippers, without a muffler and without the endless paraphernalia of Prudence — of that Prudence which is so pleased with itself when it has wriggled its way into being called Shrewdness. This author does not accept the enormous commonplace platitude — still being legislated today — according to which "one owes respect to the living and truth only to the dead." This critic believes that one owes the truth — to everyone — about everything — everywhere and at all times, and that one must cut off the hands of those who, holding truth in their hands, simply close their hands. This writer believes only in personal, irreverent, and indiscreet criticism which does not pause to dabble in frivolous or imbecile esthetics at the threshold of the conscience of a writer whose work is under scrutiny, criticism which goes into that conscience, sometimes with whip in hand, to see what is inside.[2]

Barbey owes to Sainte-Beuve the idea of seeking out the man behind the work, but that is where the similarities end. Barbey could not brook Sainte-Beuve's extreme suppleness, the countless nuances and half-tints, the evasiveness of a mind which expresses itself best in a sinuous style. Barbey had greater appreciation for Taine's systematic thinking, for its forthrightness and clarity, but remained forcefully opposed to Taine's scientific determinism. Barbey's criticism is like no other, for it is profoundly personal and vehemently polemical in the name of the Cross and the Crown, so that the symbols he found most appropriate were "a pair of scales, the sword and the cross."[3] Criticism, according to Barbey, was the Bench where literary works were to be judged ruthlessly, particularly from a moral point of view; indeed, he often professed his scorn for criticism which avoided moral issues. A critic, he insisted, must be authoritarian, dogmatic, uncompromising, free from obligations to any clique or coterie in order to insure his integrity and his total independence. He must use his writings as a weapon in defense of Truth, not tolerating sophistry or falsehood in any form; but he must also teach, he must strive to educate public opinion. In addition to being a sentry, a judge, and an executioner, the critic should be a "seer," combining intuition with his powers of observation, using also the physician's ability to dissect and the historian's talent for situating a work or an author in a broad intellectual and cultural context.

To a quite considerable degree, Barbey lived up to his own conception of the critic, frequently expressing unpopular views. There is no dichotomy between Barbey the novelist and Barbey the critic, to the extent that both his fiction and his critical writings make very clear the man's quintessential opposition to many of the values shared by most Frenchmen of the nineteenth century. His abundant energy allowed him to thrive on this very basic opposition, so that he never seemed to weary of denouncing the mediocrity of his era, the *gravité* of the bourgeois, the intellectual dessication brought about by the excesses of rationalism. Over and over, he inveighs against moderation (*le juste milieu*) as a spurious bourgeois value, or against sentimentality, deism, religiosity — various manifestations of weakness, he thought. Complacent optimism à la Renan, unlimited faith in humanity, and impassivity in literature were other *bêtes noires*.

Both his enemies and his admirers would agree to these basic points; hence his detractors have had an easy time making of him a ludicrous anachronism or a thoroughly forbidding figure. But in truth Barbey is far more flexible and human than his perfervid proclamations of orthodoxy would lead us to believe. Passionate, impulsive, abhorring weakness and moderation, he consistently responded with enthusiasm to whatever expressions of passion or violence he encountered in literature. He was therefore fascinated by Diderot,[4] drawn to Stendhal's cult of energy and to the haughty pride and satanism of Byron's heroes, arguing that any true portrayal of vice in whatever form bears an implicit condemnation of vice. He extolled wit, sparkle, and brio wherever he found them. As an early defender of reverie, mystery, the supernatural, he deserves to be considered a forerunner of Symbolism. The vigor of his thought and style, the depth and accuracy of his insights, the originality and independence of his views, his persistent ability to surprise his reader, all of that makes for provocative reading. Even today, he does not leave us indifferent, and he is seldom dull. His essays on Flaubert, Hugo and Zola are still infuriating; but he was among the very first to recognize the greatness of Balzac, Stendhal and Baudelaire — a fact which in itself suggests extraordinary powers of discernment. The rest of this chapter will show Barbey at his best and also at his worst, by summarizing his views on some of the better-known writers of the nineteenth century.

II *Balzac*

If one is to believe Barbey, there is not a single talent lacking in Balzac, a great poet — in the traditional sense of "maker" — and a powerful thinker with a perfectly integrated world-view. With his epic faculties, Balzac goes well beyond the pettiness of "art for art's sake" (which Barbey detested), practicing art for the sake of truth as defined by the teachings of the Catholic Church. Architect, painter, sculptor, Balzac had a prodigious gift for setting in motion an entire civilization around a given character. Without wincing, Barbey proclaims that Balzac is the Shakespeare of France,[5] stating categorically that "Balzac, as much as Shakespeare, has the faculty for inventing or remembering impressions, which is often the entirety of human creativeness; [Balzac also has] the gifts of observation and intuition which are nothing more than lightning-like observation, passion and color (its offspring), and above all wit, which crowns and scents genius with its lightest flower and its most penetrating perfume! Balzac has all of that, just as much as Shakespeare, but in addition, he has a host of nuances which Shakespeare did not have and could not have known, coming as they do from a much more refined civilization and education than those of Shakespeare..."[6] In declaring Balzac to be the greatest writer in the history of world literature, Barbey was not seeking to ingratiate himself with an influential writer, since Balzac was long since dead, nor was he being as chauvinistic as he might appear. Barbey sincerely believed in the inherent superiority of the novel over drama, because in the latter neither analysis nor description were possible. Shakespeare was therefore at a disadvantage and was further handicapped by his lack of a cohesive, all-inclusive vision of creation. Barbey insisted that Shakespeare did little more than express, albeit brilliantly, his multitudinous impressions, whereas Balzac's ideas of universal order and unity were obvious throughout *La Comédie humaine*. It is Barbey at his idiosyncratic best.

III *Stendhal*

In 1853, Barbey announced that Stendhal was the greatest observer, writer and artist of the century, after Blazac. It is a formidable tribute and came several decades before Stendhal's true stature began to emerge, so that Barbey was among the very first of "the happy few" for whom Stendhal had written. The tribute appears surprising if one compares the philosophical and religious beliefs of the two, for one is at the opposite end of the spectrum from the other. Barbey was strongly attracted by several aspects of Stendhal, especially by his refusal to conform, to have his behavior determined by the whims of style or public opinion; he found inexhaustible charm in Stendhal's writings, piquancy and sagacity in the man who had understood — before Barbey himself — the real depths of dandyism. Stendhal was "naturally aristocratic, as one must be, when one is born a Duke," Barbey wrote in his masterful review of Stendhal's *Correspondance* in 1856,[7] a review well worth taking into account before dismissing Barbey the critic as an anachronism:

Regardless of his opionions and principles, Stendhal was a man, intellectually, and that suffices for criticism to be concerned with him, out of a literary interest and even in the interest of morality. Moreover, it must be admitted, one is not free to ignore him. Portraits of the doges are veiled only when they have been decapitated. Not only does Stendhal have the unquestionable merit which forces the hand of criticism, but he has, in addition, a unique fascination which obliges us to consider him. The character of this false or sincere mind (and for us he lacked sincerity) is to have the attraction of an enigma. "He is the palace in the labyrinth," about which a woman of genius once spoke. He was molded in contrasts and his iron will remolded them in him. A materialist without bombast, subterranean, closed, he had throughout his life that awful simplicity of deep error which, according to the Church and its terrifying language, is the sign of final impenitence. But this materialist had seen war, that great school of sacrifice and of scorn for matter. He had seen war, had waged war and the healthy smell of gunpowder had preserved the vigor of his mind, if not of his soul, from the final decay of corruption. He was a man of action, the son of an age which had been action itself, bearing upon its thought the reverberation of Napoleon. He had touched that magic steel wand called the sword — which one never touches with impunity. He had kept something military in his thought, and something like a black necktie which contrasts strongly with the gaudy genius of literatures of decadence.

The passage points up yet further aspects of Stendhal's genius which help explain Barbey's admiration: strength and vigor, extremely rare, according to Barbey, in nineteenth-century France, and also a newness, an originality which compels Barbey to state that "one is not free to ignore him." The passage amounts to a recognition that Stendhal is a force to contend with in French literature, a "lion in the path" that must be dealt with, as Henry James later said about Maupassant. The doubt regarding the sincerity of Stendhal's beliefs indicates Barbey's genuine discomfort vis-à-vis those beliefs; and the doubt itself, though unpleasant, detracts very little from the otherwise unequivocal praise. The image of "the palace in the labyrinth" suggests the depth of that praise; for the image was first applied to Barbey himself by the sister of Maurice de Guérin, and Barbey delighted in the compliment. There is, finally, admiration for the man of action which historical circumstances prevented Barbey from being, and admiration for the disciplined nature of Stendhal's writing. In short, the piece goes far in explaining why Stendhal remained Barbey's "intellectual depravity."[8]

IV *Hugo*

Barbey's treatment of Victor Hugo amounts to an unfortunate case of blind intransigence modified somewhat by occasional moments of fairness; the various articles on Hugo also reveal Barbey's considerable capacity for viciousness. Writing about *Les Contemplations* in 1856,[9] Barbey declares that one must hurry and speak about the work because it will soon be forgotten. Victor Hugo has progressed since his previous works, but the progress has been in the direction of the absurd, the empty, the alienated and the monstrous. After thus outlining Hugo's evolution, Barbey sets forth an extremely lofty conception of poetry, justifying the traditional reference to poetry as "the language of the gods," and setting up modern poetry as the opposite of what once was a sublime form of art; Victor Hugo exemplifies this product of the modern age, with typical grossness and unutterable turgidity. Barbey seems to find pernicious delight in accumulating invectives, discovering symptoms of elephantiasis, every manner of exaggeration, blasphemy, incoherence, "anarchy of the mind raised to its highest power." Victor Hugo is machine-like, an indefatigable maker of verses, and the work as a whole is qualified as chaotic and grotesque; only the section entitled "Pauca meae" is excepted from generalized abuse, and one wishes that — in the interest of fairness — Barbey had dwelt on the real merits of that part of the work.

In his 1859 review of *La Légende des Siècles,*[10] Barbey strikes a
more positive note, proclaiming that the dying poet of *Les Contemplations* has resurrected, showing a more intense life than ever
before. The critic detects progress toward maturity, refers to Victor
Hugo as an "eternal lyric poet," asserts that the poet is, in his very
essence, a primitive beyond his time, in a period of decadence, in
love with all that is primitive, such as strength, in its most physical
and brutal manifestations. Victor Hugo is a man of the Middle
Ages:

He is a genius who, by his very nature, belongs to us Christians, people of
the past, historical minds, and who, by betraying us, betrayed himself
even more than us. This imagination, fortunately indomitable, despite its
strange trappings and its almost shameful cavessons, refused to remain
what God had made it for His glory and for its own. This imagination
transformed itself into a blind despiser of the past which still gives it its talent even when it debases that past while portraying it! Yes, the entire question, the only question which Criticism must ask Monsieur Hugo is: What
has the modern era given him in exchange for the talent he has sacrificed to
it?

To avoid any possible ambivalence, Barbey answers the question by
urging the reader to compare the finest pieces of *La Légende des
Siècles,* all of which were inspired by the Middle Ages, to those inspired by the modern age, with its humanitarianism, its belief in
pantheism and in progress. The rift between Barbey's religious,
political and social ideas, and those of Victor Hugo was simply too
great for Barbey to be fair; yet he concludes his article with laudatory and optimistic words, inspired by Victor Hugo's loyalty to the
Muse: "He has remained faithful, valiant, indefatigable, fertile, of
that tenacious fertility which is a sign — the sign of sovereignty in
the vocation of creative writing — and for that reason he may be
the only one today who can give us, after powerful works, that pure
masterpiece which is the last word of a man or of a century."
    In 1862, Victor Hugo is taken to task for *Les Misérables,* in a
series of essays[11] which would make us suspect Barbey of bad faith,
if we were not well acquainted with his extremism and his habit of
following his ideas to their logical conclusions. After decrying the
pretentiousness of Victor Hugo's undertaking, namely the attempt
to write a prose epic of the nineteenth century, Barbey attacks the

work on decidedly ideological grounds: "Monsieur Victor Hugo, the former Olympio, asking — not very olympically — asking socialism the honor of being its novelist and its poet...." The book is neither a failure nor a platitude, but a sophism and the most dangerous book of the age, Barbey charges, for it argues that humanitarianism must replace penal legislation. The danger, inherent in the idea itself, is enhanced by Victor Hugo's bold exploitation of it, by his vigor and resoluteness; and Barbey deplores the degradation, the vulgarization of a once proud talent. He is downright maddening when he reproaches the author for allowing his Bishop, Bienvenue, to retain the morality of the Church after rejecting its dogmas. He vociferates against the melodrama, the literary sansculottism, the amphigory which he finds in the work whose characters, except for Javert, are mere caricatures.

Fortunately for his own reputation as a critic, he does point out the work's stylistic merit, "all that inflamed materiality of words and images which one is free not to like, but whose power one feels." Thanks to this style, says Barbey, Victor Hugo avoids the sad destiny of being a mere imitator of Eugène Sue. He simply will not accept Hugo's evolution away from the medievalism which has served him so well in the past, he will not reconcile himself to Hugo's "democratic" ideas, viewing him as a has-been, a literary ex-emperor who abdicated to become a champion of popular rights. After stating that there are two ways of arriving at falseness, he proclaims quite dogmatically that Victor Hugo, "ever the sovereign, has mastered both of these supremely well." One might expect this attack to represent the height of exacerbation in Barbey's career as a critic, but he had even more vitriolic words for Zola.

V *Vigny*

Unwilling to look beyond his own political beliefs in order to assess properly the true genius of Victor Hugo, Barbey demonstrated much more critical acumen in his articles on Vigny, seeing in his poetry a *suavité* reminiscent of Racine's.[12] *Eloa* constitutes the very essence of Vigny's poetry, according to Barbey, who was moved as much by the beauty of the poetry as by the boldness of the ideas it expressed: "Divine generosity is interpreted by the most touching of human generosities. The sublimity of goodness conceived is almost equal to the sublimeness of the goodness of action." He was considerably less enthusiastic about Vigny's historical novel, *Cinq-Mars,* which pales when compared to the works of Walter Scott; and in this same article, Barbey sets forth his own conception of the historical novel: "...one must refrain from placing in the forefront a well-known story about which Reverie, like Curiosity, has exhausted itself; one must rather use such a story as background, in the fecund, softening vapor of distance for a different story — invented — with its series of incidents and its procession of characters."[13]

The posthumous publication of Vigny's *Les Destinées* in 1864 drew from Barbey a glowing tribute to the man with a supreme and calm distinction and to his poetry:

In an age when poetry has become so external that its entire soul has been externalized and the plasticity of Rubens is the common goal of all poets, there is nothing more curious or unexpected than these few verses, which have not gushed forth, but have dropped slowly from a thoughtful mind, as blood drops slowly from a wound when it is too deep to discharge. And that is not all. In an age when those poets who are the most Christian by their inspiration, introduce into their poetic Christianity some lax epicurean element (for even pain has its own sensuality), there is nothing more striking than to see what heretofore had not been seen: Stoicism in poetry writing for us, with the softest hand ever to have existed, verses with this virility of ideas and this simplicity of expression.[14]

The praise, quite surprising in view of the major religious differences between Barbey and Vigny, might be misinterpreted as simply part of Barbey's criticism of contemporary poetry, but an 1867 review of *Le Journal d'un poète* should dispel all doubt concerning the critic's real feelings about the poet. After asserting that the *Journal d'un poète* is the most beautiful and heart-rending book to have been published since Pascal, Barbey justifies his mention of Pascal and Vigny in the same sentence: "Both of them, except for matters of form, individual talents and vocations, belong to the same intellectual race — idealistic, religious, reflective. Some heads have been gloriously designed to break themselves uselessly against the heavens. Such was Pascal. Such was Vigny. The problem of human destiny weighs upon one as much as upon the other, and was the great suffering, the great anxiety of both.... both experienced to the same degree this particular suffering, the loftiest of all life's sufferings: mental anguish [*le mal de l'esprit*], worse than all the sufferings of sensitivity."[15]

VI *Flaubert*

That Barbey did not grasp the staggering achievement of Flaubert's *Madame Bovary* is obvious in his 1857 review,[16] and that in itself might justify questioning the competence of the critic. Flaubert was chafed by the review and never forgave Barbey; but a close look at the article does more than provide an enticing glimpse of a particular moment in literary history, it also points up Barbey's attempt at fairness. He begins by stating unequivocally that the success of *Madame Bovary* was just and well deserved, since the book was far greater than other contemporary works and had real value in itself. The novelist demonstrates power and originality well beyond the scope of other writers, whom Barbey sees as miniscule when compared to Balzac and Stendhal, of whom they are merely servile imitators. Yet *Madame Bovary,* according to the critic, lacks tenderness, poetry and what he calls *idéalité,* and therein lies the reason for Barbey's incomprehension. He simply cannot fathom the clinical approach to a fictional study of the human heart, the complete impassivity of the novelist in the face of the most passionate or moving situations: "He is indifferent to what he writes with the scrupulousness of love. If, in Birmingham or in Manchester, they manufactured, out of good English steel, machines to narrate or to analyze which would run automatically by some unknown technique of dynamics, they would function absolutely like Monsieur Flaubert does. You would feel in those machines as much life, soul and human guts as in the man of marble who wrote *Madame Bovary* with a pen of stone, a pen comparable to the crude knives of savages."

Flaubert is not immoral, Barbey declares emphatically; he is merely insensitive. For Barbey, it is inconceivable that a novelist could remain so resolutely indifferent toward a character he has created; writers either extol the virtues of their characters or deplore their failings; in either case, they become involved. Flaubert's failure to become involved is precisely what grates on Barbey the most; just as Emma Bovary lacks feeling for her child, likewise her author lacks feeling for her — and that, in Barbey's opinion, is a radical flaw. *Madame Bovary* has unquestionable power, but it suffers from a fundamental dryness, a lack of enthusiasm, and cruel cold-bloodedness. To be sure, Flaubert arouses and satisfies the reader's curiosity; but he does not have that charm, the ability to bewitch the reader, which is the hallmark of true art.

The article is far from being totally negative, as the above already indicates, and it does contain a substantial amount of praise. Barbey affirms, for example, that Flaubert has not succumbed to the banal temptation of writing a thinly disguised autobiographical novel, as so many would-be novelists are wont to do: "Monsieur Gustave Flaubert belongs to the race of real novelists, for he is an observer more concerned with others than with himself." Barbey praises the author again by stating that he has portrayed a type of woman "forgotten by Balzac" — Balzac, the greatest of all novelists for Barbey. The latter is mistaken however when he sees in Emma Bovary the average woman of civilizations grown old, the embodiment of banality and mediocrity. Barbey's failure to recognize Emma's superiority over the prodigiously banal milieu in which she is compelled to live, his failure to empathize with the gap between the enticements society has proffered her through literature and the preposterous platitude of her everyday world, these failures are quite simply beyond comprehension.

Barbey himself suffered all his life from a similar dichotomy between dreams and reality and from a similar ennui. That his dreams were of a different order than Emma's or that he became a "productive" member of society instead of committing suicide does not alter the simple fact that he did not grasp the essential nature of the female Quixote. Yet, Barbey does credit Flaubert for having understood Emma Bovary and for having treated her with appreciable depth.

He regrets that Flaubert has not applied the same piercing vision to other members of the little society at Yonville-l'Abbaye, blind again to the real differences between Bournisien and Homais, for example, and to the acute vision to which both bear witness. Flaubert is praised for a style which is one "of a literary artist who has his own personal style, colored, brilliant, dazzling, and of an almost scientific precision." The "stone" he had referred to earlier is often a diamond, Barbey now states; but a diamond, despite its brilliance, is hard, monotonous, and does not lend itself to expressing nuances. Emphasizing Flaubert's microscopic vision, he makes the rather amusing remark that the novelist is "an entomologist of style, who would describe elephants exactly as he would describe insects."

Barbey's article on *L'Education sentimentale* reveals his scorn for both the author and the work.[17] In his article on *Madame Bovary*, he had alluded to the coldness of Goethe and it is again the seeming lack of emotion, the absence of enthusiasm and passion which blind Barbey to the greatness of *L'Education sentimentale*. The love which lasts a lifetime, the chronicle of a turning-point in French history, the virulent social criticism, all of that is lost on Barbey. He sees here nothing but vulgarity and exasperating detailed descriptions, and takes Flaubert to task on both counts. In the process, he summarizes his own views on Realism: "I know perfectly well that the Realists, of whom Monsieur Flaubert is the right hand, state that Monsieur Flaubert's chief merit is *to be vulgar* [*faire vulgaire*], since vulgarity does exist. But the error of Realism, that vile school, consists in perpetually viewing *precise rendering* as the goal of art, which should have but one goal: Beauty, and since the manner in which one portrays it does not ennoble it, manner simply cannot make vulgarity beautiful." On this point, literary history has proven Barbey wrong, of course; yet Barbey also vociferated against another tenet of Realism and was vindicated by far more than literary history. The French Realists had proscribed the use of heroes, along with the very notions of the heroic and the ideal, wishing to replace all of that with the banal, the commonplace and the vulgar. Obviously, Realism has made invaluable contributions to literature and the other arts, but twentieth-century literature has restored its rightful place to the ideal and the heroic.

VII *Baudelaire*

The article Barbey wrote on *Les Fleurs du Mal*[18] is among the most enthusiastic and perceptive he ever wrote. Several times I have referred to Barbey and Baudelaire as kindred souls; and the 1857 essay on *Les Fleurs du Mal,* rejected by *Le Pays,* and subsequently included in the "Articles justificatifs" submitted by the poet's attorney during Baudelaire's disgusting trial, indicates to what degree the critic understood the poet. The article bears testimony to the soundness of Barbey's judgment, it offers an insightful reading of the work, and it is an homage to Baudelaire's genius. It is necessarily defensive, since the puritans of the day were besieging the

poet with accusations of pornography; yet the defensive note does
not take away very much from the critic's perspicacity.

Barbey makes statements about Baudelaire's poetry which could
readily be applied to his own novels, especially regarding the
work's morality: "Monsieur Baudelaire's book is not *The Flowers
of Evil,* it's the most violent extract ever taken from these accursed
flowers. The torture which such a poison must produce saves you
from the possible dangers of intoxication." Barbey's main argument consists in asserting that the work contains a condemnation
of the vices and evil it evokes, a condemnation which takes the
form of punishment after crime, disease after excess, remorse, sadness, ennui, the degrading shame and suffering which devour us:

God is infinite talion. One has willed evil, and evil engenders. One has
found the poisonous nectar to be good, one has taken such a dose, that
human nature cracks and dissolves completely. One has sown the bitter
seed, one reaps the deadly flowers. Monsieur Baudelaire, who has gathered and collected them, did not say that these *Flowers of Evil* were beautiful or that they smelled good, that one had to decorate one's forehead with
them, or fill one's hands with them, and that therein lay wisdom. On the
contrary, while naming them, he stigmatized them. At a time when sophistry strengthens cowardice and when everyone is the doctrinaire of his
vices, Monsieur Baudelaire has said nothing in favor of the vices he so
energetically molded in his verses. He will not be accused of having made
them attractive. They are hideous, naked, trembling, half-devoured by
themselves, as one imagines them to be in Hell.

The critic advances other arguments meant to emphasize the
work's morality, sometimes using purely esthetic phenomena
toward that end, stating for example that Baudelaire is a "dramatic
poet," an actor playing the role of the sophist or of the corrupt
individual. The development of this idea leads Barbey to some of
his more intriguing remarks:

He played a role, but he played it in that bloody comedy of which Pascal
speaks. The profound dreamer dwelling in the heart of every great poet
wondered in M. Baudelaire what poetry might become if it went through a
mind organized, for example, like that of Caligula or Heliogabalus, and
the monstrous *Flowers of Evil* blossomed forth for the instruction and
humiliation of us all. For it is far from useless to know what can flourish
in the manure of the human mind decomposed by our vices. It's a good
lesson. However, through an inconsistency which concerns us and whose

cause we know, there are, mixed in these poems, the cries of a Christian soul, yearning for the infinite, cries which destroy the unity of this terrifying work and which Caligula or Heliogabalus would never have uttered; only from the poet's personal point of view would this be construed as an imperfection. Christianity has penetrated us to such an extent that it distorts even our conceptions of willful art, in the most energetic and obsessed minds. Even if one is the author of *The Flowers of Evil* — a great poet who does not consider himself a Christian and who, in his book, positively does not want to be a Christian — one does not have eighteen hundred years of Christianity behind oneself with impunity.

Barbey himself might have used the argument about role-playing in reference to his own works. The narrators he creates for his tales about bewitched or diabolical women allow him the delights of making outrageous remarks concerning sex, lust, or passion, while disowning these same remarks as coming from reprobates. Barbey, too, wondered what might issue forth from minds with strange configurations (Sombreval — the married priest — or any of his diabolical women) — not to extol such behavior, but certainly to exploit it esthetically, as did Baudelaire.

One also recognizes in the works of both Baudelaire and Barbey the anguished quest for the infinite, the muffled agony of the outcast crying out to Heaven for an end to suffering. Whether in the *Fleurs du Mal* or in *Les Diaboliques,* eighteen hundred years of Christianity are deeply felt. It would be difficult to overemphasize just how compatible Baudelaire and Barbey really were. They attained similar depths of exasperation, anguish and pessimism; they shared a deep knowledge of *la littérature satanique,* and Barbey aptly pointed out that in this area, Baudelaire had made previous works seem quite elementary with his "universal erudition of evil." Barbey proved to be prophetic when he stated that Baudelaire's talent itself was "a flower of evil blooming in the hothouse of a decadence," almost as if, in 1857, Barbey had foreseen the literature of the *fin-de-siècle,* most commonly referred to as "decadent" literature.

Barbey makes many other probing comments on *Les Fleurs du Mal.* He touched upon an essential aspect of Baudelaire's genius when he stressed the importance of sensation in Baudelaire, stating categorically that the poet had explored sensation to its extreme limit, as far as that mysterious door to the infinite, which he found no way of opening. Barbey singled out "La Charogne" as "the only spiritualist poem in the collection," a truth one is not likely to discover for oneself. Whether through intuition, shrewdness or simply after careful re-reading, Barbey detected, in *Les Fleurs du Mal,* the existence of an "architecture secrète" — the phrase originated with Barbey — which gave significance to the precise place occupied by each poem, while giving solid unity to the collection as a whole. In addition, there are these penetrating comments:

There is indeed some Dante in the author of *The Flowers of Evil,* but Dante of an age of decadence, atheistic and modern, Dante coming after Voltaire, in an age when there will be no Saint Thomas Aquinas. The poet of these *Flowers,* which ulcerate the bosom where they rest, does not have the grand mien of his majestic predecessor, and it is not his fault. He belongs to a troubled, skeptical, mocking, nervous era, wriggling in ridiculous hopes of transformations and metempsychoses; he does not have the faith of the great Catholic poet which gave him the august calm of security amid the sorrows of life. The character of the poetry in *The Flowers of Evil,* except for a few rare pieces which despair finally froze, is uneasiness, fury, the convulsed look, and not the somberly clear, limpid look of the Visionary of Florence. Dante's Muse saw Hell dreamily, that of *The Flowers of Evil* breathes it in with a contorted nostril like that of the horse sniffing gunpowder! One is returning from Hell, the other is headed there. If the first is more august, the other is perhaps more moving.

VIII   *Zola*

In 1873, Zola published *Le Ventre de Paris (Paris's Belly)* in which "Les Halles" (The Central Markets), as the main figure, are endowed with life, and in which the author flawlessly captures the reality and the atmosphere of the area around the Halles, an area teeming with activity. The work is best remembered for the "poetry" of its descriptions, for its fusion of Naturalism and Impressionism, for its attempt to transpose an inherently non-poetic reality into art. *Le Ventre de Paris* elicited from Barbey one of his most vituperative articles, a review which shows the man at his acrimonious best; for in this novel he foula a perfect foil.[19] While it is generally true that the man defined himself by his opposition to the nineteenth century, it is particularly true of his response to Zola. He excoriates the novelist for having enshrined pork-butchery as the idea of modern times, for having written words deprived of a soul, and denounces Realism as the bastard child of materialism and democracy. There is nothing here to praise and everything to condemn:

In this most elaborate novel, all the pretensions, all the flaws, all the vices, all the manias and, even worse, all the ties of the putrid School to which the author belongs are pushed, by a man not lacking in vigor, to the last degree of acuteness, exasperation, systematization, obstinacy and folly. One finds here all the refuse which is dear to *them* [the Naturalists]. They have their own well-known theories concerning the end of art in the manner of Raphael and Michelangelo, harking back to the age of popes and kings, theories on the beginning of a new art, the art of the future, industrial and atheistic, conceived by the abject minds of the contemporary era! There is the sumptuous love of vulgarity and baseness which distinguishes these Sansculottes of Realism, in open revolution against all that is not vulgar and base like they are, and which would make them paint the dejections of humanity with singular pride! Finally, there is ... the pork-butcher! the pork-butcher who removes art, from the lofty and noble spheres where it should reside, into the pork-butcher's shops and who poses the insolent, barbaric and filthy axiom that "henceforth, that is where one must look for Beauty and for its laws!"

The Naturalists were looking for Beauty with a hook, Barbey declares, a sure way of not finding Beauty and of wanting a good hook. Granting that Zola does have talent, he predicts an early end to his writing career unless he makes an about-face instantly, because he has reached an extreme limit, "he is on the edge of the pig's trough of Realism, in which he can easily drown. Unfortunately, as I am fully aware, he is magnetically attracted to that trough. Pigs excite him. He shares the opinion of Monsieur Victor Hugo, that powerful poetical swineherd who was not afraid of writing: 'I called the pig by its name, — why not?'" Perhaps the most biting sarcasms are those applied to what has often been referred to as the "symphony of cheeses," that well-known impressionistic description of cheeses. The critic quotes long excerpts from the selection, adding his own reactions in parentheses; reading this part of the article is akin to hearing Barbey reading the selection himself and commenting on it spontaneously. A brief example follows:

All around them, the cheeses stank... (What a solemn beginning!). Next to the pound-breads, in beet-leaves, a cantal cheese was sprawled out, as if

split open with an axe; then there was a gold-colored cheshire cheese, a
gruyère looking like a wheel fallen off some barbarian's chariot (beautiful
and glorious, for a piece of cheese!), some Dutch cheeses, round like cut
off heads (which must make them appetizing!), smeared with dried blood,
with the hardness of empty skulls, from which they derive their names of
têtes de mort (that really completes the picture!).

When Zola published *La Faute de l'Abbé Mouret* in 1875,
Barbey saw *Le Ventre de Paris* in a somewhat different light. The
latter work could be dismissed as the rather gross fancy of a mind
without taste willing to face possible disgust and scorn, but ending
up inspiring both — in sum, a nauseous joke. Barbey considered *La
Faute de l'Abbé Mouret* a serious frontal attack against Catholicism and felt compelled to use other weapons besides jeering and
mockery, though these too are used, so contemptuous was he of
Zola.[20] He debunks the alleged novelty of Zola's stated aim to give
art a scientific base, arguing that Zola was merely imitating Balzac,
while distorting Balzac's ideas in the process. He faults him for
seeking to eliminate spirituality from literature as well as from life,
and attributes the novel's success to Zola's hatred of Catholicism,
which forms the substance of the work, and to the baseness of its
inspiration. Zola has deliberately set out to dishonor the typically
devoted, pious priest, establishing a false equivalency between
mysticism and idiocy, states Barbey. In the critic's opinion, Zola
sees the real sin of l'Abbé Mouret to be his chastity before his fall
and his subsequent repentance. L'Abbé Mouret commits the vulgar, facile sin so often ascribed to priests by the most commonplace
critics of the Church, according to Barbey, who denounces Zola's
bad faith for denying any real struggle on the part of l'Abbé
Mouret and for omitting the tragic dimensions such a story must
have. Barbey does not believe that the modern age has produced a
book whose inspiration has been more base:

It's the apotheosis of universal rutting in all of creation. It's the diviniza-
tion of the beast in man, it's the copulation of animals all along the line,
with a technique of expression heated by the desire to produce an effect,
which must be Monsieur Zola's grand desire, and perhaps his only one.
That's what gives this book its own particular indecency. With the eighteenth century behind us, we had seen every manner of indecency. We've
had naïve indecency, voluptuous indecency, naughty indecency, cynical

indecency. But we were lacking scientific indecency, and it's Monsieur Zola who has the honor of giving it to us.

The success of *La Faute de l'Abbé Mouret* drives Barbey to some doomsday conclusions about the modern world: "One can boldly state that there is no longer any literature here, just a bit of literary tinsel intended to decorate but not to conceal the filthy Materialism which is pushing us all toward the sewer where all the old nations go to rot. When such books are read and are successful, there is no more criticism to be written. There is a page to write about the mores and the history of the society which reads them."

About Barbey's review of *L'Assommoir*[21] nothing needs to be said except perhaps that the critique is even more vitriolic than those just discussed. Barbey's exasperation reaches paroxysmal proportions; the words *fange* (mire), *bourbier* (mud-pit) and *ordure* (filth) abound, and Barbey's thought is best summed up in his reference to Zola as "a grimy Hercules who stirs up Augeas' manure and adds to it." No understanding would ever be possible, if only because of the subject matter Zola had chosen and with which he dealt tirelessly in novel after novel. Quintessential differences between the two writers left them bitter enemies to the very end.

IX *Huysmans*

A Rebours (Against the Grain), published in 1884, is a landmark document in the literary career of Huysmans and in the French nineteenth-century novel. It signals the author's break with Naturalism, it represents one of the few Symbolist fictions, and it captures the very spirit of what is called Decadence in French literature — an admixture of artificiality, satanism, eroticism and religion, with strong sado-masochistic overtones. Barbey had personal reasons for being pleased by *A Rebours*, for it appeared to justify his opinion of Naturalism as a dead-end; moreover, Huysmans had expressed in his work deep admiration for *Un prêtre marié* and for *Les Diaboliques*.[22]

"*Against the Grain!* Yes! against the grain of common sense, of moral sense, of nature, such is this book, which cuts like a razor — through the inept, impious platitudes of contemporary literature." The sheer originality of the novel (one could have predicted it) partly explains the enthusiasm of the critic who, for several years, had not found cause for much enthusiasm. Barbey's fervor, however, goes well beyond mere rejoicing over Naturalism's loss of an adherent; he is responding to the specific originality of the novel:

Monsieur Huysmans' hero ... is sick like all the fictional heroes of this sick age. He has fallen prey to the neurosis of the century. He belongs in the Hôpital Charcot. A fictional hero in good health, enjoying all his faculties in their full harmony is something rare, almost a phenomenon. The phenomenon used to exist. Passion — which is what novels are about — used to unsettle that equilibrium and alienate man's freedom, without suppressing it. Nowadays, it has been suppressed. Of all the freedoms in which people pretend to believe, they believe least in freedom of the soul. Nowadays, before being passionate, one is sick.

Barbey's lifelong obsession with psychological and physiological anomalies has been emphasized during the course of the present study; but now Huysmans is stating that the anomaly has become generalized, it has become the norm. In making this kind of statement about the age in which he lived, Huysmans could count on Barbey's approval for two major reasons. Barbey would, of course, praise almost anyone willing to vituperate the nineteenth century; in addition, Des Esseintes can easily be seen as a distant relative of Barbey's own fictional characters, many of whom also live against the grain of "common sense."

According to the critic, despair is the moving force behind Des Esseintes, whom he sees as a weakling in his futile attempts to alter the nature of life. As such, the novel might not offer any reason for applause, but throughout his piteous efforts, Des Esseintes suffers irremediable torture, a sense of the agonizing uselessness of his efforts. Above all, the author of *A Rebours* has an apocalyptic vision which coincides with that of Barbey himself:

Monsieur Huysmans' book is not the story of a decadence of a society, but of the decadence of humanity as a whole. In his novel, he is more Byzantine than Byzantium itself. Theologastric Byzantium believed in God, since she discussed His Trinity, without having the perverse pride of wanting to remake the creation of the God in Whom she believed. This old, inept lover of mountebanks and coachmen demeaned and debased herself to the level of those small things in which peoples who once were great finally die, and who, when they are old, stoop down to the ground, but she did not fall into things as miniscule as those invented by a novelist bored by God's creation!

Barbey is most sensitive to the despair, the agony, the ennui, the anguish suffered by Des Esseintes: he had undergone enough of all that himself to empathize, and to believe that it left the author but two choices, suicide or prayer, as he had stated in his review of *Les Fleurs du Mal.* Faced with such a limited choice, would Huysmans opt for the religious solution, as Barbey so fervently hoped? The critic astutely points out that *A Rebours* closes with a prayer, since Des Esseintes has recognized the emptiness of his revolt against life: "Ah — said he — my courage fails me and my heart is sick within my breast ... Lord, take pity on the Christian who doubts, on the unbeliever who would like to believe, on the galley slave of life who embarks, in the night, beneath a sky no longer lit by the consoling beacons of hope!"

X Conclusion

The foregoing should suggest the nature and the tone of Barbey's criticism. Hating the nineteenth century with passionate fervor, he poured much of his hatred into his reviews of contemporary literary works. The mediocrity of the books he was compelled to judge as a professional critic for various newspapers merely added to his exasperation. It mattered not at all that any critic in any age has to deal with mediocrity much more than with excellence — such arguments never impressed Barbey, for they did not alter the essence of his task. Yet, for all of that, he cannot be called a negativist, because he constantly sought for areas of possible agreement and reasons for enthusiastic praise in the works he reviewed. At least once, the search proved fruitful, and we have seen the frenzied praise he lavished upon Baudelaire. In the closing years of his life, he had the consolation of writing about other like-minded writers, younger men like Huysmans, Maurice Rollinat and Jean Richepin. That he went on seeking out talent till the very end suggests very strongly that beneath the exasperation there was hope.

CHAPTER 6

Conclusion

W HILE every writer of note is Janus-faced, looking backward to his intellectual masters, to some definite, recognizable tradition, and at the same time facing the future, anticipating it to some degree, the phenomenon seems intensified in the case of Barbey. His masters were Joseph de Maistre, Balzac, Lord Byron and Walter Scott; one also suspects that the works of Sade left a deep impression on him. His influence is, at the very least, just as improbable as the diversity of his masters, since this "Holy father of the Decadent movement"[1] is generally considered the first Catholic novelist in French literary history. That he is France's first major regionalist writer also adds to his uniqueness. The more salient elements of this strangeness will be briefly summarized in these concluding pages.

In Barbey's highly personal world-view, human solitude is the most basic "given," and becomes an all-pervasive theme in his works. Most of his characters are isolated from one another; they revolt against this condition, striving to break out of the jail cell of solitude, usually by means of passion. The individual invariably fails in the endeavor and is thrown back into a worse solitude, for he now knows that it cannot be broken. This human isolation is irreversible, it has strong metaphysical overtones, and death provides the only escape. Passion does offer a provisional escape, without being more than a reprieve, orchestrated by an ironic, almost sadistic Fate. The great triumph would be to create a permanent *solitude à deux,* but this is achieved only once in all of Barbey's stories. There is a concomitant isolation, wrought by historical circumstances upon the few survivors of the provincial aristocracy; this is a haughty kind of isolation, accepted as the only worthy attitude in a time of apocalyptic change.

Passionate love is most commonly associated, in these stories, with suffering, cruelty, religion, and death. Love can reveal latent masochism, transforming a young man into the willing victim of a female vampire, as in *Ce qui ne meurt pas*. The evolution of Barbey's stories shows a growing concern with physiological and psychosomatic manifestations of destructive passions; passion first undermines the victim's psyche before poisoning the body, as in *L'Ensorcelée*. The ultimate phase is death, either through suicide, slow deterioration, or trauma. Paradoxically, what inspires passion can be, and often is, ugliness and decay: it is the beauty of the Medusa sung by Shelley. Indeed, Barbey specializes in the monstrous, the bizarre, the exceptional, so that one thinks of Caligula enraptured with a statue of Diana which accompanied him wherever he went. In many instances, the links between love and hate are strong; the "partners" engage in a combat which gives every sign of being mortal, and each one enjoys it enormously. For Ryno and Vellini (in *Une vieille maîtresse*), hate is always ready to surface, even during their most passionate moments.

Except in Barbey's early novels, passion does not exist outside of a religious context. Passion as a source of depravity on a purely human plane is also the source of eternal damnation; certain characters scoff at religion in the name of love, with varying degrees of lucidity, thus lending credibility to the thought that men enjoy most that which damns them. The association of passion and religion is most clearly seen at the linguistic level, with religion used as a source of imagery to describe the workings of passion, quite as if religious terms were the most adequate means of evoking passion, and thus transgression is compounded. For passion itself is forbidden by Barbey's Jansenistic God, and the religious imagery employed to evoke passion constitutes a second transgression, so that we witness a sacrilegious *sacralisation* of passion. Sacrilege and blasphemy abound in these stories, with most characters in open revolt against God; the conscious, deliberate and clearly articulated preference for passion over the promise of Paradise, eternal damnation used as a backdrop for a forbidden love affair, the vocabulary of religion applied to the phenomena of sex and passion, such is the general thrust of the use Barbey made of sacrilege and blasphemy. It is all a part of his work, as essential to it as the Norman landscape.

Religion and passion are virtually inseparable in these works. Elaborate descriptions of religious ceremonies suggest the appeal of ritual and pageantry. There is something of the religious esthete in Barbey, but it remains far less developed than in the works of Chateaubriand or Huysmans. He prefers to dramatize the most negativistic, the most draconian of the Church's teachings, making Eternal Reward an unattainable goal for even the least fiery or passionate of God's creatures. He then sets in motion the *most* passionate beings, condemning their sins while remaining secretly fascinated by them and by their maniacal rush toward eternal self-destruction. Yet the issue here transcends the commonplace belief of vice punished and virtue rewarded, for many of these stories raise the ever-relevant question about whether human lives are governed by free will or by fate. The issue is not quite as obfuscated by satanism as one might be inclined to believe; for Barbey's satanism, when it is not part of the legends and superstitions of Norman lore, usually functions as an indication of absolute passion seen as absolute evil.

Almost as powerful as his fascination with sin was Barbey's intense cult of the past. He never ceased regretting the powerlessness of the collective past over the present and repeatedly expressed his nostalgia for the chivalric and heraldic golden age of the French monarchy. Barbey knew he was witnessing the demise of the aristocracy, a former symbol of strength now in its final hour, and brought to this juncture not solely by historical forces beyond control, but by the personal degeneracy, abuses and excesses of the nobility itself. Barbey had the lucidity to recognize, and the integrity to admit, that those who had been born to govern were weakened, victimized, and laid low by their own vices. He viewed his own age as one of decadence, as the end of a world, the end of centuries-old traditions and values. An entire world-order had been obliterated and Barbey felt he was contemplating the smoking ruins of a city in which precious little had survived: here and there a descendant of an aristocratic family, who had kept alive the memory of vanished strength, glory and power. For this reader, Barbey's quest of things past does not appear excessive; it is, rather, a welcome antidote to future shock and to that myopic cult of the present which consigns to oblivion anything "older" than today's newspaper. Barbey's work bespeaks the need for roots, traditions and what is called "cultural heritage" in every human being.

The *fantastique* in Barbey's works is intimately linked with his regionalism; it is used to suggest a mood, to conjure up an atmosphere, but also to evoke the more obscure regions of the human soul, the twilight zone of irrational obsessions or neurotic fears. One must keep in mind Barbey's contention that the belief in legends and superstitions, in a century of materialists and positivists, was the privilege of an elite. Moreover, Barbey himself never doubted the intervention of obscure, evil powers in human affairs. His use of the *fantastique* is merely an expression of his anti-materialist, anti-rationalist views, for reason and matter could not satisfy his curiosity about life. It is indeed true that he offered psychological explanations for strange behavior patterns, but it remains for the reader to choose between the psychological explanation and the *fantastique,* i.e. the supra-rational. For Barbey at least, life had a spiritual dimension which the writer must take into account.

His criticism of Parisian society can be as intriguing to twentieth-century readers as it was for his contemporaries. With good reason, he denounces the cynicism of a libertine and blasé society which has ceased believing in sincerity and which has created its own moral code through its cultivated contempt for love. Thus, the Parisian *haut monde* hypocritically prohibits the open expression of authentic love. Love in marriage does not exist, because marriages are arranged between families, or else they are *mariages de raison* pure and simple. Religion, too, prohibits extra-marital love and would seem to be conspiring with the social code to stultify or eliminate passion from the lives of passionate beings. Since passionate love obviously appeals to most mortals, and since the forbidden fruit has appealed to men and women from time immemorial, the confluence of the religious taboo and the social taboo appears to be a cunningly calculated way of ensuring the perpetuation of passionate love. In seeking to fulfill his desires, however, the individual is compelled, by religion and society, to mask his innermost self. Barbey has handled most deftly this dichotomy between appearance and reality, showing the explosiveness lying beneath the cool, tranquil façade of propriety. The individuals Barbey chose to unmask were selected in keeping with his interest in the bizarre and the exceptional, in keeping too with his fascination with the advances made by men such as Claude Bernard and Jean Martin Charcot. As a result, Barbey's novels and stories offer an unbalanced portrait of certain aspects of nineteenth-century France, but there is merit in his uncanny ability to explore some of the outer-most reaches of human experience. These are areas less remote, to be sure, than those seen by Baudelaire or Rimbaud; yet they are far removed from the commonplace, hence they still appeal to the un-common reader.

There is obviously much anguish in Barbey's writings, and con-siderable anxiety, along with a heightened awareness of the immi-nence of death — death without serenity. But the writings also con-tain hope. Although he agonized over the passing of the old aristoc-racy, Barbey noted the emergence of a new aristocracy, character-ized by beauty or strength, rather than by noble birth. Louis Tainnebouy in *L'Ensorcelée,* Calixte Sombreval in *Un prêtre marié,* Hauteclaire Stassin in "Le bonheur dans le crime," Mesnilgrand in "A un dîner d'athées," all of them exemplify strength or beauty, either in the physical or in the moral spheres. This is one way of positing that the man who defined himself by his permanent opposition to the nineteenth century could yet find hope for his contemporaries and for their successors.

True, the essence of his message deals with the impossibility of significant and lasting human communication, particularly be-tween male and female, but the quest for communion goes on throughout life. The tragedy of Barbey's characters was to seek in the "other" an Absolute, unmindful or unaware that the "other" can never be Absolute. They are frenzied, passionate, extremely impatient characters, and they very much remind us of our own contemporaries who also want an Absolute instantly and forever in the here and now. In addition, Barbey's stories are more than par-ables about human solitude — although as such they excel — for beneath the seemingly outdated trappings, the reader finds precious insights into the minds and hearts of the old nobility. Barbey takes us beyond snobbery and the sense of caste to the innermost recesses of these largely forgotten people, showing us their instincts, their loyalties and their disintegration: it is the nobility approaching, then reaching its final hour.

As a storyteller, Barbey is quite simply a virtuoso. As a thinker, much of what he has written may seem dated, but the previous paragraphs should indicate that even here he cannot be dismissed lightly. When he repeatedly emphasizes, for example, the extreme age of the nineteenth century, he gives us pause, inviting self-questioning about our own century. He has also associated religion with eroticism to a degree which will require far more probing studies than have yet appeared. Nor have we exhaustively analyzed his contribution to what might be called "medical realism." In literary history, he has few disciples; yet Verlaine acknowledged him as a master, and Barbey was admired by Huysmans, Montesquiou and Proust. For Léon Bloy, he was a mentor. For the "Decadents" — Huysmans, Rollinat, Richepin, Péladan and others — his works were a major source of inspiration. His novels and stories are at the origin of the Catholic novel in France — a tradition which includes Bloy, Bourget, Bernanos and Mauriac. For Barbey's readers in the twentieth century, the following words, written by Remy de Gourmont, have proven prophetic: "Barbey d'Aurevilly is one of the most original figures in nineteenth-century French literature. It is likely that he will long excite curiosity, that he will remain one of those singular and subterranean classics who are the real life of French literature. Their altar is at the far end of a crypt, but the faithful descend to it willingly, while the temple of the great saints stands openly in the sun, with all its emptiness and its ennui."[2]

Notes and References

Chapter One

1. Barbey d'Aurevilly, *Oeuvres romanesques complètes* (Paris: Gallimard, 1966), II, p. 565. All quotations from Barbey's writings are taken from this two-volume "Bibliothèque de la Pléiade" edition (1964–1966), except where otherwise noted. Subsequent pagination is included parenthetically. Translations from the French are mine throughout.
2. The exact importance of Normandy in the works of Barbey has yet to be adequately assessed. The debate still goes on as to whether he is or is not an "écrivain normand."
3. Barbey d'Aurevilly, *Lettres à Trébutien* (Paris: Bernouard, 1927), III, p. 237.
4. *Ibid.*, p. 287.
5. *Ibid.*
6. Quoted by Jacques Petit in his *Barbey d'Aurevilly critique* (Paris: "Les Belles Lettres," 1963), p. 105.
7. *Lettres à Trébutien*, III, p. 64.
8. *Ibid.*, p. 274.
9. In a letter to his mother, dated Aug. 11, 1862.
10. Quoted by André Bellessort in his "Barbey d'Aurevilly," *Le Supplément Illustré de la Revue Hebdomadaire*, V (May 2, 1931), p. 66.
11. Baudelaire, *Oeuvres complètes* (Paris: Gallimard, "Bibliothèque de la Pléiade," 1954), p. 1261. The reader may also wish to consult Jacques Petit's "Baudelaire et Barbey d'Aurevilly," *Revue d'Histoire Littéraire de la France* (avril–juin 1967), pp. 286–95.
12. Barbey d'Aurevilly, *Le XIXe siècle* (Paris: Mercure de France, 1964), I, 206.
13. See Philippe Berthier's "Stendhal," *Revue des Lettres Modernes,* Nos. 234–37 (1970), pp. 25–61.
14. *Lettres à Trébutien,* III, p. 334.
15. Barbey d'Aurevilly, *Disjecta Membra* (Paris: La Connaissance, 1925), I, p. 5.
16. See Barbey's *Lettres à Léon Bloy* (Paris: Mercure de France, 1903).
17. These articles were later published in volume form and entitled *Goethe et Diderot* (Paris: Lemerre, 1913).
18. *Barbey d'Aurevilly critique,* p. 408.

19. A facsimile of this letter appears in the "Classiques Garnier" edition of *Les Diaboliques* (Paris: Garnier, 1963), facing page xxvi.

20. Barbey d'Aurevilly, *Lettres intimes* (Paris: Edouard Joseph, 1921), p. 279.

21. Quoted by Albert Thibaudet in his *Histoire de la littérature française de 1789 à nos jours* (Paris: Stock, 1936), p. 383.

22. Joseph de Maistre, *Lettres et opuscules inédits* (Paris: 1851), I, p. 145.

23. Barbey d'Aurevilly, *Philosophes et écrivains religieux* (Paris: Amyot, 1860), p. 308.

Chapter Two

1. The basic works on dandyism include Baudelaire's short essay, "Le Dandy," in his *Curiosités esthétiques;* Jacques Boulenger's *Sous Louis-Philippe: Les dandys* (Paris: Ollendorff, 1907); Elizabeth Creed's *Le Dandysme de Jules Barbey d'Aurevilly* (Paris: Droz, 1938); and Simone François' *Le Dandysme de Marcel Proust* ("De Brummell au Baron de Charlus") (Bruxelles: Palais des Académies, 1956).

2. Elizabeth Creed, *Le Dandysme de Jules Barbey d'Aurevilly* (Paris: Droz, 1938), p. 121.

3. *Lettres à Trébutien* (Paris: Bernouard, 1927), II, p. 76.

Chapter Three

1. Among the numerous essays on the role of Normandy in Barbey's works, the following should be singled out for special mention: Jacques Petit, "La ville-prison"; Pierre Leberruyer & Jacques Petit, "Les eaux-mortes"; Pierre Leberruyer, "Les landes, paysage d'angoisse"; all of these appeared in *La Revue des Lettres Modernes,* Nos. 137–140 (1966). See also: Pierre Leberruyer, "Pâtres, mendiants et sorciers," *La Revue des Lettres Modernes,* Nos. 162–165 (1967).

2. Baudelaire, *Journaux intimes* in *Oeuvres complètes* (Paris: Gallimard, Bibliothèque de la Pléiade, 1954), p. 1211.

3. *Une vieille maîtresse* in *Oeuvres romanesques complètes,* I, p. 475. Subsequent references to the novels discussed in this chapter will be to this edition and will be cited in the text. Translations are mine throughout.

4. Jacques Petit, "*'Le rêve endormi des plaisirs fabuleux...,'* l'inceste et l'androgyne," *La Revue des Lettres Modernes,* Nos. 162–165 (1967), p. 62.

5. See Robert Cornilleau, *Barbey d'Aurevilly et la médecine* (Paris: Spes, 1933), p. 63 *passim.*

6. Jean-Jacques Lefrançois & Jacques Petit, "Les thèmes physiologiques," *La Revue des Lettres Modernes,* Nos. 162–165 (1967), pp. 36–37.

7. *Ibid.*, p. 37.

8. J.-K. Huysmans, *A Rebours* (Paris: Fasquelle, 1961), p. 200-1. Other perceptive remarks on *Un prêtre marié* are to be found in Léon Bloy, *Ecrits inédits* (pp. 48–89) in *Oeuvres complètes,* VIII, (Paris: Bernouard, 1948); Pierre Klossowski, *Un si funeste désir* (Paris: Gallimard, 1963), pp. 89–119; Joyce Oliver Lowrie's chapter on Barbey in her *The Violent Mystique* (Genève: Droz, 1974).

9. B. G. Rogers, *The Novels and Stories of Barbey d'Aurevilly* (Genève: Droz, 1967), p. 104.

10. Concerning Barbey's interest in medicine, the following are of considerable interest: Robert Cornilleau, *Barbey d'Aurevilly et la médecine* (Paris: Spes, 1933); Bernard Demontrond, *La culpabilité dans l'oeuvre de Jules Barbey d'Aurevilly* (Paris: Dactylo-Sorbonne, 1962); Jean-Jacques Lefrançois & Jacques Petit, "Les thèmes physiologiques," *La Revue des Lettres Modernes,* Nos 162–165 (1967), pp. 33–50.

11. *Lettres à Trébutien,* III, p. 334.

Chapter Four

1. *Oeuvres romanesques complètes,* II, p. 1290. Subsequent references to the stories and novels discussed in this chapter are included parenthetically within the text. Translations are mine throughout.

In the interest of clarity and brevity, I have taken certain liberties with regard to the locus of these stories and the identification of the person to whom the story is directly told. Although not referred to by name, the little Norman town where four of the *Diaboliques* take place has long been recognized as Valognes, beyond any reasonable doubt, and I am taking this as a given. Also, most of the *Diaboliques* are tales within a tale, with a well identified narrator relating a story either to a group or to a single listener, with the latter often reacting to the tale in progress; this single listener is referred to as Barbey throughout this discussion.

2. Léon Bloy, *Propos d'un entrepreneur de démolitions* (Paris: Stock, 1925), p. 127.

3. Barbey d'Aurevilly, *What Never Dies,* translated from the French by Sebastian Melmoth [Oscar Wilde]. (Privately Printed, 1928), p. xiii.

Chapter Five

1. Two outstanding studies have appeared on this subject: Gisèle Corbière-Gille, *Barbey d'Aurevilly critique littéraire* (Genève: Droz, 1962) and Jacques Petit, *Barbey d'Aurevilly critique* (Paris: "Les Belles Lettres," 1963).

2. Preface to *Les Philosophes et les écrivains religieux* (Paris: Amyot, 1860).

3. The significance of these symbols is discussed by Gisèle Corbière-Gille in her *Barbey d'Aurevilly critique littéraire*, p. 72.

4. See his *Goethe et Diderot* (Paris: Lemerre, 1913).

5. See his "Shakespeare et ... Balzac" in *Portraits politiques et littéraires* (Paris: Lemerre, 1898), p. 1 *passim*. Concerning Barbey and Balzac, see Hermann Hofer's "Présence de Balzac," *Revue des Lettres Modernes*, Nos. 234–37 (1970), pp. 81–119.

6. *Ibid.*

7. The article appeared in the July 18, 1856 edition of *Le Pays* and was reprinted in *Les Romanciers* (Paris: Amyot, 1865). It is included in Volume I of Jacques Petit's selection of Barbey's critical writings, *Le XIXe siècle* (Paris: Mercure de France, 1964), pp. 113–22.

8. In a letter to Trébutien dated 20 June 1855. On the question of Barbey and Stendhal, see Philippe Berthier's "Stendhal," *La Revue des Lettres Modernes*, Nos. 234–37 (1970), pp. 25–61.

9. See his articles in *Le Pays*, June 19, 1856 and June 25, 1856, reprinted in *Les Poètes* (Paris: Amyot, 1862). Excerpts are included in Jacques Petit ed., *Le XIXe siècle*, Volume I.

10. *Le Pays*, November 29, 1859. *Les Poètes*, p. 35 *passim*. Excerpts appear in Jacques Petit ed., *Le XIXe siècle*, I.

11. *Le Pays*, April 19, 1862 and July 14, 1862, reprinted in Barbey's *Victor Hugo* (Paris: Crès, 1922) and in part in Jacques Petit ed., *Le XIXe siècle*, I.

12. *Le Pays*, May 8, 1860. *Les Poètes*, p. 49 *passim*, and Jacques Petit ed., *Le XIXe siècle*, I.

13. Jacques Petit ed., *Le XIXe siècle*, I, pp. 266–67.

14. *Le Pays*, January 31, 1864. *Les Poètes* (Paris: Lemerre, 1889), p. 345 *passim* and Jacques Petit ed., *Le XIXe siècle*, II, pp. 39–41.

15. Jacques Petit ed., *Le XIXe siècle*, II, pp. 94–96.

16. *Le Pays*, October 6, 1857. *Les Romanciers* (Paris: Amyot, 1865). Jacques Petit ed., *Le XIXe siècle*, I, pp. 205–13.

17. *Le Constitutionnel*, November 29, 1869. *Le roman contemporain* (Paris: Lemerre, 1902). Jacques Petit ed., *Le XIXe siècle*, II, pp. 156–63.

18. *Les Poètes* (Paris: Amyot, 1862), p. 371 *passim*. Jacques Petit ed., *Le XIXe siècle*, I, pp. 198–204.

19. *Le Constitutionnel*, July 14, 1873. *Le roman contemporain* (Paris: Lemerre, 1902), p. 197 *passim*. Jacques Petit ed., *Le XIXe siècle*, II, pp. 214–22.

20. *Le Constitutionnel*, April 20, 1875. *Le roman contemporain* (Paris: Lemerre, 1902), p. 213 *passim*. Jacques Petit ed., *Le XIXe siècle*, II, pp. 253–59.

21. *Le Constitutionnel*, January 29, 1877. *Le roman contemporain* (Paris: Lemerre, 1902), p. 230 *passim*. Jacques Petit ed., *Le XIXe siècle*, II, pp. 277–79 contains short excerpts.

22. *Le Constitutionnel,* July 29, 1884. *Le roman contemporain* (Paris: Lemerre, 1902), p. 271 *passim.* Jacques Petit ed., *Le XIXe siècle,* II, pp. 338–43.

Chapter Six

1. Mario Praz, *The Romantic Agony* (London: Collins, The Fontana Library, 1960), pp. 345–46.

2. Remy de Gourmont, *Promenades littéraires* (Paris: Mercure de France, 1922), I, p. 258.

Selected Bibliography

(Unless otherwise specified, place of publication is Paris.)

PRIMARY SOURCES

1. In French (sets)

Oeuvres complètes, 17 volumes, Bernouard, 1926–27. This edition does not include any of Barbey's critical writings, but it does contain the four volumes of the *Lettres à Trébutien.*

Les Oeuvres et les Hommes, 26 volumes, rpt. Geneva: Slatkine Reprints, 1968. Most of Barbey's literary criticism is subsumed under this general title.

Oeuvres romanesques complètes, ed. Jacques Petit. 2 vols. Gallimard, 1964–66. (Bibliothèque de la Pléiade.) The most authoritative edition to date of the novels and stories. Contains excellent Introduction, as well as a critical apparatus for each of the works. Includes *Du dandysme et de George Drummell* and Barbey's journal, the *Memoranda.*

2. Editions in French of the Major Novels

Le Chevalier des Touches, Preface by J.-P. Séguin. Garnier Flammarion, 1965.

Les Diaboliques, ed. J.-H. Bornecque. Garnier, 1963. (Classiques Garnier.)

L'Ensorcelée, ed. Jacques Petit. Garnier-Flammarion, 1966.

Un prêtre marié. Preface by Pierre Klossowski. Club Français du Livre, 1960.

Une vieille maîtresse, ed. Jacques Petit. Livre de Poche, 1968.

3. Editions in French of Other Works

Articles inédits. Les Belles Lettres, 1972.

Le XIXe siècle. ed. Jacques Petit. 2 vols. Mercure de France, 1964–66. (Excerpts from Barbey's critical writings, preceded by an overview of Barbey's criticism.)

Premiers articles, ed. Andrée Hirschi & Jacques Petit. Les Belles Lettres, 1973.

Les Prophètes du Passé. Palmé, 1880.

177

Les quarante médaillons de l'Académie, ed. Gilles Rosset. Pauvert, 1966.

4. English Translations

The Anatomy of Dandyism, with Some Observations on Beau Brummell, trans. D. B. Wyndham Lewis. London: Peter Davies, 1928.

The She-Devils (Les Diaboliques), trans. Jean Kimber. Intro. by Enid Starkie. London: Oxford University Press, 1964.

A Story Without a Name, trans. Edgar Saltus. New York: Brentano's, 1919.

What Never Dies, trans. Sebastian Melmoth [Oscar Wilde]. Paris: Privately Printed, 1928. (Contains Preface & Introduction by "Sebastian Melmoth.")

SECONDARY SOURCES

1. General Works

BÉSUS, ROGER. *Barbey d'Aurevilly.* Paris: Editions Universitaires, 1957. A brief, lively account of the man and his work.

CANU, JEAN. *Barbey d'Aurevilly.* Paris: Robert Laffont, 1965. A leisurely biography, well documented and nearly exhaustive.

COLLA, PIERRE. *L'univers tragique de Barbey d'Aurevilly.* Bruxelles: La Renaissance du Livre, 1965. An in-depth, thought-provoking study of Barbey's obsessions.

DUMESNIL, RÉNÉ. *Le Réalisme et le Naturalisme.* Extremely insightful, short presentation (pp. 59–78).

PETIT, JACQUES. *Barbey d'Aurevilly critique.* Paris: Les Belles Lettres, 1963. Indispensable. Goes well beyond the scope suggested by the title and contains much biographical data.

ROGERS, B. G. *The Novels and Stories of Barbey d'Aurevilly.* Geneva: Droz, 1967. Offers a close reading of all the major works.

2. Specialized Studies

BORÉLY, MARTHE. *Barbey d'Aurevilly maître d'amour.* Paris: Editions "Les Marges," 1934. Important contribution to an understanding of Barbey's lifelong preoccupation.

BOUCHER, JEAN-PIERRE. *Barbey d'Aurevilly: Une esthétique de la dissimulation et de la provocation.* Montreal: Presses de l'Université du Québec, 1976. Provides a detailed study of the *Diaboliques.*

CORNILLEAU, ROBERT. *Barbey d'Aurevilly et la médecine.* Paris: Spes, 1933. Excellent study of a central feature of Barbey's fiction.

CREED, ELIZABETH. *Le dandysme de J. Barbey d'Aurevilly.* Paris: Droz, 1938. Still the best study of this complex aspect of the man and his works.

DEMONTROND, BERNARD. *La culpabilité dans l'oeuvre de Jules Barbey d'Aurevilly.* Paris: Dactylo-Sorbonne, 1962. A psychiatric study of the theme of guilt in Barbey's fiction.

LOWRIE, JOYCE O. *The Violent Mystique: Thematics of Retribution and Expiation in Balzac, Barbey d'Aurevilly, Bloy and Huysmans.* Geneva: Droz, 1974. A probing look at the themes of transgression and atonement in the major novels.

SCHWARTZ, HELMUT. *Idéologie et art romanesque chez Jules Barbey d'Aurevilly.* München: Wilhelm Fink Verlag, 1971. Underscores the essential relationship between these two aspects of Barbey's work.

YARROW, P. J. *La pensée politique et religieuse de Barbey d'Aurevilly.* Genève: Droz, 1961. A good synthesis of a complex subject.

NOTE: *La Revue des Lettres Modernes,* in its "Barbey d'Aurevilly" series, has published eight volumes (1966–1974), containing substantive articles and updated bibliographies, along with many previously unpublished documents.

Index

(The works of Barbey d'Aurevilly are listed under his name)